A Formula for Conversation

Christians and Muslims in Dialogue

Livingstone A. Thompson

UNIVERSITY PRESS OF AMERICA, ® INC.

Lanham • Boulder • New York • Toronto • Plymouth, UK

Copyright © 2007 by
University Press of America,® Inc.
4501 Forbes Boulevard
Suite 200
Lanham, Maryland 20706
UPA Acquisitions Department (301) 459-3366

Estover Road
Plymouth PL6 7PY
United Kingdom

Library of Congress Control Number: 2006938324
ISBN 0-7618-2886-9 (paperback : alk. ppr.)

ISBN-13: 978-0-7618-3638-4 (clothbound : alk. paper)
ISBN-10: 0-7618-3638-1 (clothbound : alk. paper)
ISBN-13: 978-0-7618-3639-1 (paperback : alk. paper)
ISBN-10: 0-7618-3639-X (paperback : alk. paper)

$\bigotimes^{TM}$ The paper used in this publication meets the minimum
requirements of American National Standard for Information
Sciences—Permanence of Paper for Printed Library Materials,
ANSI Z39.48—1992

To Jean-Marie, Lesley-Ann, JoAnna and Jordana

Contents

Acknowledgements   vii

Introduction   ix

   Living in a Post-Christian Society   ix

   Plurality in Christianity   xi

   A Point of Reference for the Study   xi

   Aim and Outline of the Study   xiv

1   Starting the Conversation with Islam   1

   Speaking from a Particular Point of View   1

   Plurality and Difference in the Same Tradition   3

   The Relevance of the Bohemian Formula   4

   Christian-Muslim Dialogue   5

   Christians and Muslims in Community   7

2   A Formula for Unity and Dialogue   9

   The Emergence of the Bohemian Formula   9

   The Pre-Reformation Period   10

   The Reformation Period   12

   Comenius and the Bohemian Formula   14

   The Post-Reformation Period   16

   Towards an Inter-Faith Formula   19

3 The Essentials in Islam 25

Faith and Praxis 25

The Oneness (Unicity) of God 27

The Problem of the Trinity 30

Overcoming Disputes Concerning the Trinity 31

The Qur'an as God's Final Speech 32

4 The Qur'an and Muhammad in Islamic Piety 39

The Exemplary Role of the Prophet 39

The Qur'an and Islamic Piety 44

Conflicts Between the Bible and the Qur'an 45

5 Christian Essentials and Muslim Questions 51

The Nature of the Problem 51

The Primacy of Scripture 53

The Centrality of Jesus 56

Questions About Jesus 58

Diakonia: Christian Witness and Service 59

Taking Stock of Our Journey 61

6 Speaking of Islam: What Can Christians Truly Say 65

Speaking the Same Language? 65

Towards a Theology of Modesty 67

The Inter-faith Implication of Theological Modesty 69

Theological Modesty in the Qur'an 71

In Ignorance—Unity 72

In Faith—Proximity 74

In Christology—Difference 77

Conclusion 83

A Select Bibliography 87

Index 91

Acknowledgements

I wish to express my appreciation to my wife Jean-Marie and our three daughters Lesley-Ann, JoAnna and Jordana for their understanding and support during the research for this book, which is dedicated to them. A special word of thanks also to Thomas Minor and Otto Dreydoppel who facilitated my stay in Bethlehem, Pennsylvania and assisted me in my use of the Groenfeld Collection at the Reeves Library, Moravian College. Thanks to Professor John D'Arcy May and the Library staff at the Irish School of Ecumenics, University of Dublin (Trinity College), who gave very helpful advice and direction. Jean-Marie Thompson and Sharon Gardner read the manuscript and made helpful corrections that I would probably have overlooked. Any remaining error or omission is, however, my responsibility.

Introduction

LIVING IN A POST-CHRISTIAN SOCIETY

There was a time when we could speak of a Christian country, a Christian region and even a Christian empire but today all of that has changed. Very few countries, and certainly not those in the West, are monolithic in terms of their religious expressions. In countries and regions that were formerly referred to as Christian people of different beliefs mingle freely, as they practice their faith in the presence of each other. It is now true to say that the era of Christendom has truly passed. We are living in a post-Christian, plural age. This reality presents adherents of the different religions with significant challenges relating to the ways in which they understand themselves and how they are to live along-side each other. This book explores the question of the relation between Christianity and Islam.

The case of Christianity and Islam, the two largest world religions, is particularly noteworthy. In many countries these days it is becoming more and more likely that Christians will have Muslim neighbors. The free movement of people and the increasing respect for the free practice of religion, particularly in Western countries, is seeing to this. In many European countries with a Christian heritage Islam represents the fastest-growing religious faith community. However, it is often felt that the religions are at war with each other. In support of this perception reference is sometimes made to the fact that those involved in the activities, which eventually led to the September 11, 2001 destruction in the USA, claim to be Islamic adherents. The subsequent comment made by an America religious leader indicates how rhetoric can function to demonize a religion. According to the evangelist in question, Islam is an evil religion. However, a comment such as this can only be fair if the perpetrators of the 9-11 attacks represent the best of Islam, if any at all. Happily that is not the case because those attacks, as well as subsequent attacks in Spain and the United Kingdom, have been condemned by Muslims who feel that those responsible can find no justification in Islam for these violent acts.

This writer is convinced that for peaceful and respectful co-existence adherents of a particular religion must take time to understand the beliefs of people of other faiths, as well as their own. Part of the objective of this book, then, is to encourage Christians and Muslims to focus on and develop some appreciation of those things that are central to the practice of Christian and Muslim piety. Improved understanding will facilitate the development of rhetoric, which both Christians and Muslims find acceptable. The way Christians speak of Muslims is a case in point: in the aftermath of the New York tragedy one Muslim leader in the United Kingdom reminded his television audience that we should not speak of "British Muslims" but rather Muslims in Britain. In other words, the religion must be seen as a worldwide community with adherents everywhere and anywhere. Christianity in general, and particular Christian communities, must take account of Islam, not only because of the differences and the uniqueness but also because of the similarities. One prerequisite for understanding another religion properly is that the believer must first develop a workable and up-to-date understanding of the religion she or he is practicing. There is the need, then, for careful consideration of how the relationship between Christianity and Islam can be fashioned in terms of those things central to both faiths. There is no point trying to cover up the difficulties in saying we can just live together because we believe in the same one God. That will not help understanding because nothing can be substituted for critical appraisal. Before Christians dismiss the value of Islam, it should be borne in mind that that religious tradition provides millions of people with the means whereby they can encounter the one whom they believe to be their creator and the worthy object of their worship. This is no small issue because it means that the *raison d'être* of the religion is not to prove the untruth of Christianity. Likewise, Muslims will do their faith no credit by wishing Christianity away because the Christian faith does not exist for the purpose of fostering the demise of Islam. At their best, both faiths provide their adherents with meaning and purpose for existence. Taking an approach that suggests that one or the other is worthless will be of no help in today's plural world. At the same time, one religion is under no obligation to regard another as bring of equal salvific value, just as one Christian Church is not obliged to accept another as church in the fullest sense of the word. This brings us to the issue of plurality in the religions, which must then fashion a means of dealing with internal as well as external differences.

PLURALITY IN CHRISTIANITY

One persisting feature of Christianity is the multiplicity of its communions or denominations. Even though some argue that we are living in a post-denominational era, denominationalism is still a feature we have to contend with because millions of Christians still see themselves through the lenses of their particular account of their communal history and beliefs. It seems, though, that some communions find it easier than others do to live with people of other faiths because of their particular history and doctrinal emphases. In some respect this is true also for Islam where there are different emphases and the same weight and importance are not given to all tenets of the faith. Many Christians and Muslims have not reflected carefully on their own faith in relation to the other and so have formed and perpetuated misunderstandings, which make for poor relations. Some believers have not just refused to reflect and carefully study the other; they simply do not know where to begin and what method to use.

Nevertheless, understanding one's own faith history is critical to living peacefully with others. This book is intended to help both Christians and Muslims to develop an approach to mutual understanding and careful assessment. It, therefore, looks at the situation of the relationship between Christianity and Islam from the point of view of a particular denomination. The methodological significance of this approach cannot be overstated. When a Christian meets a Muslim, the Christian is one who has a particular faith history, who worships in a particular way and in a particular place. Likewise, the Muslim has a particular perspective on the history of his or her faith and worships in a particular way and in a particular place. Numerically speaking, there may be as many differences between two communities within Christianity as there are between a particular Christian communion and Islam. A similar claim can be made for Islam, in which there are also wide-ranging divergences. It is important, then, to have a good grasp of an approach to mutual understanding, which does not take for granted what is fundamental to each faith tradition, which is what this book aims to do.

A POINT OF REFERENCE FOR THE STUDY

Bearing in mind the assertion above that a reflection cannot take place in a vacuum, it is important to note that this study is grounded in Christian theology, as mediated through the Moravian Church. This observation is important if the reflection is to be credible and concrete in its application. The point being made by this approach is that each Christian who engages in a reflection on another faith must first clarify the understanding of the faith they have, which is communicated through a particular worshipping community. Every reflection is "a particular" reflection because it emanates from a particular perspective in a particular place and time. So when we say Christians believe and practice something, we must then ask, "Which Christians, living where and at what time? For this reason the title of the book should be understood as referring to a conversation in a specific context rather than attempting to construct a meta-narrative to suit all situations. A general position is meaningless because no person occupies such a position. Each person lives in a particular situation and has a bias, which affects the way in which opinions are developed and the way in which convictions are shaped. These, in turn will affect the approach to conversation.

There are a few other reasons why the choice of the Moravian Church as a point of reference is not to be seen as *ad hoc*. The plural nature of the Christian community, a study in which the doctrinal principles of religious communities are being discussed requires some specificity. The Moravian Church is used as the point of reference because its ecclesiology reflects a good mix of Roman Catholic and Protestant practices. It maintains much of its Roman Catholic heritage while standing at the forefront of the Protestant tradition. For example, in a manner similar to the Vatican Council, the Moravian Church has maintained a single Synod that governs the affairs of the whole worldwide communion. The three-fold form of its ministry is also similar to the form we find in the Roman Catholic, Orthodox and Anglican Churches. At the same time, however, from its understanding of the sacraments, it is the first of what can be called the Protestant Churches, having been established some fifty years prior to the Lutheran Reformation. From the point of view of Christians, the Moravian Church is important because the church carries within its history an approach to dealing with doctrinal differences that can serve the whole Christian community. This point should not be seen as a contradiction to the insistence on having a specific point of reference. The fact is that despite its Roman Catholic, Protestant and, one may add evangelical characteristics, the Moravian Church is a single communion within Christianity and does not presume to represent all of Christians.

The small size of a communion does not disqualify it from being the starting point of conversation. As with other Christian communions, the Moravian Church carries within its history aspects of the whole spectrum of the Christian tradition. This is true for any communion, which perceives itself as a point of entry for conversation with representatives from another religion. It is not usual then to say that any part of the Christian tradition, whether Roman Catholicism, main stream Protestantism or the so-called evangelical tradition can be at home in the Moravian Church.

From the point of view of Islam, a dialogue with the Moravian Church may be seen as a door of entry into the Christian tradition. Apart from the issue of its ecclesiology, dialogue with this communion will represent a move of historical import, as the communion is one of the oldest of the Protestant churches, having been established during the time of the Muslim Ottoman Empire. Moreover, long before the period of the Enlightenment, as we shall see later, Moravian theologians were working out models for relationship and dialogue with Islam.[1]

The approach to doctrine that we find in the Moravian Church history is a challenge both to Christians and to Muslims alike. For example, the early Moravian perceived that there was the need to single out those things that were necessary for salvation. In view of this, they sought to set out clearly those things in Christian thought and practice. The categories they used in developing this approach were the Essential things, the Auxiliary things and the Accidental things.[2]

The things Essential were divided into things on the part of God and things on the part of human beings. On the part of God the essential things were the grace of the Father, the merit of Christ and the gifts of the Holy Spirit. On the part of human beings the essential things were faith, love and hope. The things that were Auxiliaries included the Word of God, the keys[3] and the sacraments. These things were given as the means whereby the essentials became known: the word of God reveals, the keys assign and the sacraments seal. The auxiliaries serve the essentials to ensure that the purity of the faith was kept intact.[4] The Accidentals of Christianity were those things relating to the time, place and mode of worship, which included the ceremonies and the external rites of religion. These things, which were later called the accessories, should be practiced with liberty and prudence, and "in a manner that they might not only prove no obstacle to faith, love and hope, . . . but rather than they might serve to illustrate and impress them."[5] The Moravian argued that the Essentials and the Auxiliaries were commonly held among Christians but the Accidentals were drawn from practices in the primitive church and various indications in Holy Scripture. Although they were to be treated with a measure of flexibility, at the same time the recognition of Accidentals was not a license for individuals to change and introduce ceremonies and opinions without subjecting them to proper general examination.

By establishing a hierarchy in beliefs and practices, the early Moravians were indicating those truths they were prepared to negotiate and those that were not open for discussion. In relation to some doctrines there had to be unity among Christians, while in others liberty should be allowed. This approach to belief and practice became important for attempts at church unity in the seventeenth and eighteenth centuries.[6]

AIM AND OUTLINE OF THE STUDY

Given the demand there is for each communion to engage with the plural context, this approach to doctrine is part of the contribution that the Moravian Church can make to discussions on pluralism. Whether this approach that organizes truth in a hierarchical fashion has relevance to the present plural context remains to be seen and will be explored in what follows. The assertion being made is that this approach has application for working out the relations between different faiths in a plural context. In the reflection that follows, this writer will show how this approach to doctrine can be useful for Christians and Muslims, as they seek to develop a way to understand and relate to each other. Of necessity this study is brief because it is the starting point of a conversation. The aim is not to make an elaborate theological treatise but to provide the framework for a deeper conversation between Christians and Muslims. From the point of view of the Moravian Church, it is a retrieval of a well-used formula for re-application to a broader plural context and it may be the first time that the approach is being considered for an inter-faith conversation.

Chapters 1 and 2 set the basis for the conversation by looking at the usefulness of the formula, "In essentials, unity; in non-essentials, liberty; in all things, charity." An attempt is made to accurately locate the historical emergence of the formula. It is called the Bohemian formula because it indicates the approach to doctrine used by the early Bohemian Brethren. Chapters 3 and 4 look at the things in Islam that can be called "essentials." These include a brief look at Islamic monotheism and its implications for Christian monotheism, as well as the role of the Qur'an and the Prophet Muhammad in Islamic piety. Chapter 5 deals with three issues, the primacy of scripture, the person of Jesus and diakonia (Christian witness and service), which are essential in the practice of the Christian faith. From a consideration of the issues in the preceding chapters, chapter 6 attempts to indicate what Christians can truly say about Islam. Most importantly, this chapter introduces a theological approach called the theology of modesty, which may break new ground in the way we approach inter-faith conversation.

NOTES

1. For a detailed look at this issue see Comenius, *Panaugia*. Translated by A. M. Dobbie. Warwickshire: Peter I, Drinkwater, 1986 and Livingstone Thompson, "Harmony, Modesty, Dialogue: A Moravian Contribution towards the Development of Christian Theologies of Pluralism." (An unpublished PhD dissertation submitted to the University of Dublin, Trinity College, 2003), 152–177.

2. This hierarchical structure for doctrine pre-empted Vatican II in its emphasis on hierarchy of truths in the context of ecumenism. The Decree on Ecumenism, *Unitatis Redintegratio* declares: "While preserving unity in essentials, let all in the church, according to the office entrusted to them, preserve a proper freedom in various forms of spiritual life and discipline . . . and even in the theological elaboration of revealed truth. In all things let charity prevail." See *Unitatis Redintegratio* No.4 (my emphasis). In No. 11 the Decree declares: "When comparing doctrines with one another, they [catholic theologians] should remember that in catholic doctrine there exists an order of 'hierarchy' of truth, since they vary in their relation to the foundation of the Christian faith."

3. Although this seems to be a reference to papal authority, the translation by Seifferth places a footnote to John 20:22, which refers to the Holy Spirit. However, the Order treats the Holy Spirit as an essential, not an auxiliary. The reference to the instrumental nature of the ministry alerts us to the possibility that "keys" here is a reference to the office of the ordained ministry.

4. *Constitution of the Bohemian Brethren*, 102.

5. *Constitution*, 103.

6. Rouse, *History of the Ecumenical Movement*, 42–69.

Chapter One

Starting the Conversation with Islam

SPEAKING FROM A PARTICULAR VIEW POINT

A first step to be made in a proper interfaith conversation with Islam is for the Christian partner to occupy a specific location within the broader Christian tradition. This is another way of saying that every practice can be placed and understood within the context of a particular worshipping community and that it is not possible to think of Christianity without thinking of some concrete location in time and space. The reader must get this point very clear because when we live in a plural context, as we now do, we must resist the temptation of relativism, in which the claim is made that one can occupy a neutral ground. This is the weakness in the approach to pluralism that is represented by John Hick and Paul Knitter. According to Gavin D'Costa, the theology of religions articulated in the pluralism of Hick and Knitter ends up as a neo-pagan unitarianism. By seeking to obliterate differences and otherness, this pluralism ends up as a strong form of exclusivism.[1] Insisting on the specificity of one's point of reference, therefore, is a hedge against the slide into relativism, which is probably the most common sin in modern theologies of pluralism and interfaith dialogue. Being clear about a communion's history and self-understanding is critical because it will affect the way that that religious community negotiates its way through the diversities in the modern age.

The perspective from which this Christian reflection on Islam takes place is the Moravian Church or *Unitas Fratrum*. It currently comprises twenty Provinces throughout the world, which trace their origin to the attempts at reformation in Bohemia during the fourteenth and fifteenth centuries. The most outstanding leader of that reform movement was John Hus (Jan Hus), who was put to death by burning at the Council of Constance in 1415. Arising from the martyrdom, the Unitas Fratrum was established as a separate and independent religious community in 1457, after a period of great unrest and turmoil. The identity of the new church was hewn out of the chastening and repressive reaction of the powerful Roman Church from which it was thrown. The members of the new religious community referred to themselves as the Unity of the Brethren because they were concerned with the preservation of unanimity in faith and charity.[2]

By situating itself within the Moravian tradition, this study recognises that in doing theological reflection one cannot stand outside a given tradition or context. This fundamental principle of the methodology of this study mitigates against any charge that the choice of the Moravian Church, as a point of departure for the reflection is arbitrary. Beyond that, however, the choice of the Moravian tradition is based two other important grounds. Firstly, it is based on the view that the Church's competence for interfaith relations has not been fully explored. The Moravian Church is one of the oldest surviving churches in Protestantism and carries within its self-understanding a history of genuine commitment to other traditions. Having overcome many challenges to its identity during the seventeenth and eighteenth centuries, not unlike the challenges that plurality poses to Christianity, it may be that other traditions can learn from the Moravian approach to other religions. In any case, from a systematic theological point of view, no serious attempt has been made in the Moravian Church to undertake a full reflection of this nature. It is a task that cannot be sidestepped in the modern era. The study therefore provides an approach that can be followed in other traditions.

This original impulse of seeking unanimity is part of the enduring identity of the Moravian Church and part of the reason for using this church as a point of reference for this Christian-Muslim conversation. We mentioned in the earlier section that the foundational self-understanding of the communion is the view that Christian doctrine may be expressed as things "essential," things "auxiliary" and things "accidental."[3] This three-tiered categorization of beliefs and practices in Christianity seemed to have mutated into the expression "in essentials unity, in non-essentials liberty, in all things charity," which is used widely throughout the church today as a statement of Moravian self-understanding. In employing these categorizations, the Moravians were not concerned with establishing the essence of Christianity, as renown theologians like Schleiermacher, Newman, Harnack, Loisy, Troeltsch and Barth sought to do.[4] Rather, it was simply an attempt to situate the identity of the Moravian Church in the plural context among the other religious expressions. The leaders of the Church recognized that different churches may have different "orders" and that the ability to distinguish the essential doctrines from things non-essential is related to the stability it enjoys.[5] In other words, the stability and prosperity of a church depended on the clarity of its orders and its self-understanding. This identity that they articulated was one that the conditions of their church, then exposed to persecution, permitted.[6] Their preoccupation at the outset with stability may then be described as seeking an understanding of the church, an ecclesiology, which could prove viable in the dissentions then prevalent in Bohemia and later in all Europe. Yet they were not rigid about the order they chose because they were open to the view that Providence could offer something more perfect.[7]

PLURALITY AND DIFFERENCE IN THE SAME TRADITION

The approach to doctrine that we get in the Moravian Church is represented in the formula, "In essentials unity; in non-essentials liberty; in all things charity." In a real sense, this is a popular description of Moravian self-understanding. This formula was popularized during the Reformation period, being associated with the Reformer John Calvin, Erasmus and others, all of whom distinguished essential beliefs from non-essential beliefs in relation to the problem of unity. However, its roots lie deep within the old Moravian Church of the fifteenth century, which made a distinction between three levels of beliefs and practice. On the basis of arguments that will be advanced in due course and for ease of reference, we shall call the formula the Bohemian Formula.

The plurality within a given communion is part of the reason why religious communities are characterized by internal tensions. These tensions are indications that there is a mixture of theological resources, which can be helpful in dealing with a plural situation in the world. The way the old Bohemain/Moravian Church organized Christian doctrine was related to their awareness of differences between the Church and other communions as well as differences within its own ranks. Disagreement concerning the auxiliary and the accidental things should be no barrier to unity. In these things they included the modes of celebration of the sacraments, an issue which has been controversial since the Lutheran Reformation. However, they felt that the credibility of the faith and faithfulness to the apostolic tradition demanded unity on critical things, which they termed essential; for example the grace of God the Father and the merits of Christ the Son. The Bohemian formula, therefore, is an inter-church approach to unity within and between traditions.

In the case of the Moravian Church, the main source for the inner tension is the plurality of traditions that were formally incorporated into the Renewed Church in 1744. According to that Synod, "The renewed Brethren's Church recognizes within its life three modes of teaching Christian doctrine, which it distinguishes as the Moravian, the Lutheran and the Reformed tropus."[8] The

Synod of 1774 reaffirmed this position arguing that the entire Protestant Church, which sprang from the sixteenth century Reformation, agreed on the sole authority of Holy Scripture in matters of faith and on justification by faith. The centrality of the Scriptures was found to be consistent with the Bohemian/Moravian Brethren Church, which preceded the Reformation by some fifty years. The differences in their conception of Christian doctrine, their constitution and ecclesiastical practices, could be regarded as different ways of apprehending the one divine truth. However, in none of the three ways (*tropuses*) were subscribers required to give up their peculiar confession of faith in becoming a part of the renewed Moravian Church. The result was that the three interpretive traditions were allowed to exist side-by-side in the new union. The plurality of ways of apprehending divine truth was seen as a precious treasure to be faithfully preserved. The Moravian Church believed it should "be of service to the [whole Protestant Church] by means of this gift . . . to help it [the Protestant community] more and more fully to carry out the will of the Lord, 'that they all may be one'."[9] This belief has, no doubt, influenced the role of the Church in inter-church ecumenism. However, the different hermeneutical approaches that the three sub-traditions brought persisted for sometime, thus ensuring that there were differences and tensions in the ways in which Scripture and the wider Christian tradition were read. In the early years of the Renewed Church, Zinzendorf played a key role in developing a bias towards the Lutheran tradition, which is the reason the Augsburg Confession was declared to be the main confession guiding theological discourse.[10] In the immediate post-Zinzendorf period there was an attempt to lessen the role that one confession was perceived as playing. Consequently, the current *Church Order* lists ten different confessions to which it subscribes, though only the Bohemian Confession of 1535 can be called Moravian. It should then not be surprising that the church adopted the Bohemian formula, as being descriptive of its self-understanding.

THE RELEVANCE OF THE BOHEMIAN FORMULA

The argument here, then, is that this approach to doctrine that is outlined above is applicable to Christian-Muslim relations. The support for this is justified on two grounds. In the first place, it represents an accurate description of the way a community of Christians understand themselves. Apart from Moravians, who would be expected to take this approach, there are other Christians who rely on this self-understanding in relating to people of other faiths. Secondly, the formula contains the idea of a hierarchy of truths, an approach that gained ascendancy after the second Vatican Council. The Council's decree on Ecumenism speaks of unity in essentials while maintaining variety in the theological elaborations of revealed truth. We see also that in the Declaration of the Relationship of the Church to Non-Christian Religions, the Council applied the idea of a hierarchy of truths in describing what is believed about Islam. According to the Second Vatican Council, a hierarchy of truths is a means of ensuring that the faith can be expressed in different cultures without any separation of Christian truths from their foundation.

When we speak of the "essentials" in Islam and in Christianity, it is not an attempt to define the essences of Islam or Christianity. Rather, it is an approach in which one religious tradition gives account of the other using the terms of its own faith. Consequently, in this book there is a discussion on the oneness of God, the Qur'an as God's final speech and the exemplary role of the Prophet Muhammad as being fundamental to Muslim self-understanding. For the Christian faith, it discusses the primacy of Scripture, the centrality of Jesus and service to the world as being fundamental to a particular Christian self-understanding. This book then addresses the question of how, on the basis of the Bohemian formula, ("in essentials unity; in non-essentials liberty; in all things charity") the Christian community can come to a position on Islam.

CHRISTIAN-MUSLIM DIALOGUE

In the last two decades of the twentieth century we have seen an increased number of inter-faith dialogues. One of the problems with inter-faith dialogues is that they quickly reach stalemate because the conflicting claims about what God has revealed cannot be resolved. This book may also prove helpful to those involved in formal Christian-Muslim inter-faith dialogue. The fourth chapter is an attempt to move beyond that impasse in dialogue, in that it suggests a way of resolving the problems between Christianity and Islam that arise from their different accounts of revelation. Responding to differences in the way revelation is construed in Christianity and Islam is no easy undertaking because, as Paul Avis has shown, since the Enlightenment unanimity in the conception of revelation has not existed between Protestant theologians, let alone between Protestants and Roman Catholics. The trigger for this plurality of view on revelation was the fact that the Enlightenment's critique led to a subverting of all claims to unchallenged authority.[11] The argument made in this work is that the willingness to concede that we are really at one in our ignorance of God, prior to any claim to revelation, will make a difference for how Christians and Muslims view each other's claim to revelation. From a Christian point of view the mystery of God cannot be comprehended completely by any human mind or expressed completely in any human statement. There is a similar position in Islam, which states that only God—God alone—knows absolute truth. According to Islam, human beings possess only a superficial acquaintance with things. The view of revelation that develops from this concession of ignorance may allow Christians and Muslim to seek a better understanding of each other's claims, instead of dismissing them at the outset. The presumption of ignorance, then, may be seen as a starting point for theology as well as a starting point for better Christian-Muslim understanding. At the point of ignorance, Christian can affirm unity with Muslims. There are also prayers used in Christian worship, in which the request is made that Islam, which is proximate to Christians in the heritage of faith, they may come to a fuller knowledge of God's truth and love.[12] This modesty in relation to knowledge of truth signifies that not only Islam but also Christians, despite the revelation in Jesus Christ, need to move to a fuller knowledge of God's truth. It does not imply that in one faith God's truth is known but in the other it is not. Rather, Christians and Muslims alike, need to come to fuller knowledge of God's love and truth.

Although we can state traditional difficulties in ways that can make for some harmony between Christianity and Islam, it does not mean that all the problems of the relationship between the two traditions are thereby solved. The question remains whether the two traditions can live with the differences. One area of difference is the conflicting ways in which Jesus and the Qur'an are viewed. This has been an intractable problem in the relations between the two faiths. This book attempts to face these difficulties head on. The place that Jesus, the incarnation, and consequently, the Trinity hold in Christian piety is different from the way in which they are perceived in Islam. Even though Jesus in held in high esteem in Islam, Muslims neither share the Christian view that Jesus is incarnate God nor that he is Saviour of the world. What the book will show is that living beside each other is possible despite the difficulties associated with these differences. With the help of the formula, "in essentials unity; in non-essentials liberty; in all things charity," Christians can affirm unity in ignorance about the depth of divine mystery, proximity in faith as children of Abraham but at the same time difference in the perception of Jesus.

In order to get beyond the intractable difficulty of Christology, two truths must be recognized by Christians and Muslims. One is that Jesus is the one on whom Christian faith is built and that the Christian hope in God is through Jesus Christ as Lord. The other truth is that the Qur'an, which was revealed to Muhammad, is the means whereby Muslims have access to the truth of God's will and their hope of salvation. There seems to be no way of collapsing these two truths into one. They have analogous functions in relation to the respective faiths, which is what makes for differences between them. Unless our aim is to deconstruct the two faiths and construct one religion out of the two then these truths must be seen as mysteries that we are not yet privileged to solve—part of the secret things of the world that belong only to God. This recognition of differences in the perception of truth has promise for dialogue with other religions.

CHRISTIANS AND MUSLIMS IN COMMUNITY

Central to this study is that a modern statement on an understanding of the church cannot be silent on the question of other religions. This is especially true for Islam, not only because of its continuing growth, but also because of the claims to revelation that Islam makes. Two of the challenges faced by Christian Churches in today's multi-faith context are, (1) the development of an understanding of the church that is sensitive to religious pluralism and (2) the establishment of a more workable basis for interfaith relations. On the basis of the most recent Moravian Church Order (1998), for example, it would appear that the Church has taken no position on other religious faiths. Nevertheless, the Moravian Church has consistently refrained from developing a fixed doctrinal system, which ensures that the Church maintains flexibility in its doctrinal positions. This flexibility is expressed for example in the popular Bohemian formula. When the term "essentials" is used in this book, it refers to those things that are fundamentally related to the way in which Christians and Muslims understand themselves. One does not for a moment underestimate the difficulties involved in seeking to use an inter-church concept for interfaith application. Islam is not a monolithic religion but comprises differences not dissimilar to the differences within Christianity. Muslims live in different socio-political contexts, so one must be cautious in speaking of "essentials" in Islam. However, this approach that is proposed is justified because the formula is descriptive of the theological position of a Christian communion, which can be a model of how other communions may develop their own inter-faith theology.

In this chapter we have set out the challenges of getting the conversation started between Christians and Muslims. In the chapters below a number of tasks are attempted. After looking at the background of the Bohemian formula, "in essentials unity, in non-essentials liberty, in all things charity," we shall suggest what maintaining this implied flexibility in doctrine implies for a position on Islam. Noting the way in which the term "essentials" is used, an investigation of the "essentials" in Islam is also undertaken. Thirdly, the study considers those things that are fundamental to the self-understanding of a particular Christian community. This comparative look at the "essentials" in both religious traditions is motivated by the conviction that these "essentials" will inform the way Christians and Muslims give account of themselves and interact with each other. Finally an attempt is made here to move towards a theological statement on Islam. On the basis of the formula, "in essentials unity, in non-essentials liberty, in all things charity," there is an assessment of Islam in terms of Christian self-understanding. As the Muslim-Christian Research Group notes: "when believers of one religion seek to understand the faith of believers of another religion, they must necessarily go back to the terms of their own faith."[13] This task involves faithfulness without concessions to the essence of the message of revelation preserved within both traditions.

NOTES

1. D'Costa, *The Meeting of Religions*, 27–39.

2. *Church Constitution of the Bohemian and Moravian Brethren*, translated from the original Latin by B. Seifferth (London: W. Mallalieu and Co., 1866) p. 95

3. *Church Constitution*, 101. See below for a treatment of these terms.

4. See S. Sykes, *The Identity of Christianity: Theologians and the Essence of Christianity from Schleiermacher to Barth* (London: SPCK, 1984): John May has argued that the use of the words such as essential and central betrays a need to speak as if some timeless essence of Christianity were available to us. See J. May, "Essence—Identity—Liberation: Three Ways of looking at Christianity" *Religious Traditions # 6* (1984), 31. Gavin D'Costa sees the tendency towards essentialism in theology as a threat to dialogue. G. D'Costa, *The Meeting of Religions and the Trinity* (Edinburgh: T & T Clarke, 2000), 27.

5. *Constitution*, 99

6. *Constitution*, 100.

7. *Constitution*, 97.

8. Quoted in Results of the Synod of the Protestant Church of the United Brethren Held at Herrnhut in the Year 1848, IX, 104.

9. *Church Book of the Brethren's Unity of the British Province*, II, 9, 44.

10. In the Introduction to Zinzendorf's *Twenty-One Discourses,* the Synod of 1748 was keen to indicate the consistency of its positions with the Augsburg Confession. See for example ix-x. However, under the leadership of Spangenberg in the immediate post-Zinzendorfian period there was a trend away from some Zinzendorfian views. Instead of emphasis on the consistency with the Augsburg confession, the Synod of 1775 determined a list of essential doctrines to which adherence was expected. These were (1) Doctrine of the total depravity of humanity—that we cannot save ourselves, (2) Doctrine of the Divinity of Christ, (3) Doctrine of the Atonement—that Jesus died for our sins and was raised for our justification, (4) Doctrine of the Holy Spirit as the one who leads us to conviction of sin and to faith in Jesus, and (5) Doctrine of faith—that faith must be evidenced in obedience to God's commands. For a full discussion see Hamilton, *A History of the Church*, 216–221.

11. Paul Avis, Ed., *Divine Revelation* (London: Darton, Longmann, Todd, 1997), 45–66.

12. *Moravian Book of Worship* (Bethlehem, PA & Winston-Salem: Board of Publications of the Moravian Church in America, 1995), 7.

13. Muslim-Christian Research Group, *The Challenge of the Scriptures: The Bible and the Qur'an* (Maryknoll, NY: Orbis Books, 1989), 88.

Chapter Two

A Formula for Unity and Dialogue

THE EMERGENCE OF THE BOHEMIAN FORMULA

While the Bohemian formula, "In essentials unity, in non-essentials liberty, in all things, charity," is not a confessional statement, it is widely used in several religious settings. The formula has a curious history, a clarification of which may help us to value it a little more. In this chapter we will make a quick historical survey of it so as to verify its suitability for use in relations with people of different faiths.

The saying is popularly seen as belonging to a trajectory in the Protestant Christian tradition. The Moravian tradition in particular has claimed it, as being unique to that communion for over two hundred years. Augustus Schultz associates this motto with John Amos Comenius who lived in the seventeenth century. Writing in a 1914 publication on Moravian theology he said: "Our guiding principle is the motto of the Moravian Bishop and Educator, Comenius: 'In essentials unity, in non-essentials liberty, in all things charity'."[1] However, the formula does not appear in the Church Order of the Moravian Church (*Unitas Fratrum*), the official publication that outlines the main theological positions of the Moravian Unity. It appeared in the American editions of the Church Orders of 1907, 1911, and 1924 but it is not clear why the formula has been excluded from the official publications after 1924. Vernon Nelson suggested in an unpublished paper that the attitude towards the formula changed after an article on the formula appeared in the 1930 publication in a Moravian publication called the *Moravian Messenger*, which was the official organ of the Moravian Church in the United Kingdom.[2] In that article the writer, Blanford, noted that the formula belongs to the period of the Reformation and "has been traced to the writing of one. . . . Rupertus Melderius."[3] Blanford believes that the Moravians were mistaken in thinking that the formula was "[their] own invention and

9

property."[4] However, if the Moravians did not develop this formula then what is its origin? A Moravian origin is further questioned by the fact that it does not appear in any of the official publications of the Unity Synods of the Church. Nevertheless, the formula has enjoyed a privileged place in the piety and popular perceptions of the Church.

In the ventures during the Reformation period to find the right formulae to overcome doctrinal dissension the formula in question seemed to have offered much hope. It is probably for that reason why Blanford associates it with the Reformation. Since we are concerned with the effectiveness of the formula as an approach to doctrinal difference, it would be helpful to see how it was used in that period. This investigation should give some clarity about the route of the formula to its present standing and the reason for its subsequent popularity in at least one section of the Christian tradition. In so doing, we will also establish whether the pre-Reformation Moravian Church is in any way associated with it. The point of this investigation is to establish the suitability of the formula and its applicability to an interfaith situation.

THE PRE-REFORMATION PERIOD

In discussing the attempts at union between the enclaves of Christianity, Stephen Charles Neill said that it is unlikely that lasting union can be achieved, if there were not some flexibility on both sides in a dialogue, and a preliminary agreement that certain things may be treated as unessential, disagreement regarding them being no barrier to spiritual union.[5] Neill captures the genius of the formula in question very well in this observation. He centres his attention on the need to make a distinction between things necessary for Christians to hold from those that are not; a distinction between what is needed for salvation and the self-understanding of a religious tradition and the things that are not.

One of the earliest allusions to the formula that we can find is in the Pre-Reformation period of the Moravian Church. For the sixty years between the time of the founding of the Church in 1457 and the inauguration of the Lutheran Reformation 1517, the Church had the practice of making this distinction between necessary and non-necessary things. In a document called *The Apology* of 1503,[6] one of the oldest existing documents of the Moravian Church, the distinction was said to be needed because of the general confusion prevailing throughout the church.[7] In *The Apology*, distinctions are made between three orders or levels of beliefs and practice in the life of the church. A distinction was made between things "essential" (*essentialia*), things "auxiliary" (ministrative, *ministerialia*) and things "accidental" (*accidentialia*).[8] The categories of "auxiliary" and "accidental" have no exact parallel in the formula in question. What the early Moravians meant by "auxiliary" would not be equivalent to what was later called "non-essentials." Nevertheless, the main point is that there was a clear demarcation of the "essentials." The distinction between things essential to salvation and things ministrative, that is, serving the "essentials," together with the further delineation of things that are merely "accidental" "may be called the formal principle of the [early] Moravian theology."[9] The category "hierarchy of truths," which came into currency after the Second Vatican Council was anticipated in the Unitas Fratrum for over four hundred and fifty years. It is recognized that where this distinction is made today there are different understandings as to what is an essential. For example, some of the religious groups within Christianity would say that speaking in unknown tongues, or baptism, is a necessary prerequisite for salvation. However, in early Moravian theology, these things would be considered either auxiliary or accidental to the essentials.

This three-tiered hierarchical system may have been derived from an interpretation of the biblical text in 1Cor 13:13. This is evident from the catechism for children published under the title, "*EIN CHRISTLICHE UNTTERWEY-SUNG DER KLAYNEN KINDER JM GELAUBEN, DURCH EIN WEYSZ EINER FRAG. M.D.X.X.I [I]*. When translated this means, "Christian Instruction in the Faith, in the Form of Questions, for Little Children. 1522."[10] In response to the question, "Upon what does thy salvation depend?" the catechism gives the answer, "Faith, love and hope." It then quotes 1Cor 13:13 as proof and support. "And now abides faith, hope and charity, but the greatest of these is charity."[11] The remainder of the catechism is constructed on an explication of faith, love and hope. In the dealing with hope we see again allusions to the hierarchy as follows:

> 68. In what does true hope consist?
> In God essentially, in Christ meritoriously, and in the Holy Ghost and His gifts which renders us worthy of a participation (in grace); in faith fundamentally; in justification by faith truly; in works confirmingly; in the Church and its ministrations administratively; in the Word of God instructively; in the sacraments sacramentally, as a testimony and a testament.[12]

It seems also that the doctrinal distinction in the Moravian Catechism of 1522 was an appeal to early Christian authority. The reference to "essentials," "auxiliary" and "accidentals" is an allusion to expressions we find, for example, in Augustine. Augustine held that things that are called essences or substances admit of accidents, whereby a change, whether great or small, is produced in them. According to him, there can be no accident of this kind in respect of God. Therefore He who is God is the only immutable substance or essence, to whom certainly Being itself, whence is derived the term essence, most especially and most truly belongs.[13] Again we find in Augustine a commentary on 1Cor 13:13 that is similar to the way in which the Moravians used it in their Catechism. Giving pre-eminence to faith, hope and charity, Augustine wrote:

> For as the pious faith has no desire to exist without hope and without charity, it is needful that the faithful should believe what he does not yet see in such a way that he may hope for and love a vision of it.[14] . . . For where are those three things, for the building up of which in the mind the whole apparatus of the divine scriptures has been erected, namely faith, hope and charity (1 Corinthians xiii, 13), except in a mind believing what it does not see, and hoping and loving what it believes?[15]. . . . As then you see what was made as one thing, so be you one, by loving one another. By holding one faith, one love [and one] undivided charity.[16]

This evidence of Augustinian thought among the earlier Moravians is not surprising because John Hus, whose life as well as martyrdom gave rise to the Unitas Fratrum, was significantly influenced by Wyclif who himself borrowed from Augustine.[17] Moreover, Augustinian thought is said to have dominated western thought for several centuries.[18] The evidence suggests that Moravians were drawing upon a long Christian tradition, in the way in which they developed their distinction, which was weighted in terms of the importance that they placed on particular doctrinal beliefs and practice. It is difficult then to argue for an absolute Moravian originality in this distinction between things essential for salvation and things that are not.

Rudolf Rican has argued that the origins of the Bohemian Formula could be in Scholasticism. In this system of thought from the Middle Ages, there was a line of thought in which a distinction is made between the essence of the sacraments (*substantia sacramenti*) and the things that occurred, *i.e.* accidental, with the administration of the sacrament.[19] In the administration of the sacraments, the Dominican, Michael Gorranus, also made a distinction between the things that were incidental, *accidentialia* and the essentials.[20] In other words, there are precursors to the Moravian application of the idea. Yet despite these precursors, it would seem that the Moravians did not simply copy a medieval or early church tradition, but by detailing the distinctions, they gave a new thrust and significance to them, thus preserving in their own history the unique demarcation of what constitutes essential doctrines and things necessary for salvation. This demarcation became even more significant in the Reformation, the period to which we now turn.

THE REFORMATION PERIOD

One of the tasks of this section is to see whether categories "essentials," "auxiliary" (or ministerial) and "accidentals" that we find in Moravian usage in the earlier periods and the categories "essentials" and "non-essentials" that we find in the Reformation period can be used interchangeably. In this investigation Vernon Nelson, to whom we referred earlier, may be helpful. He agrees with the clergyman William Leslie Bowles that the earliest reference to the formula is to be found in Melanchthon in the form: "in necessary things, unity; in doubtful things, liberty; in all things, charity."[21] Nelson further states that the earliest authenticated use of the words of the formula is in the rare 1626 work of a Lutheran theologian, Rupertus Melderius, entitled *Paranesis.* The Latin version of the formula used by Melderius is: "Si nos servaremus in necessariis unitatem, in non necessariis libertatem, in utrisque charitatem, optimo certe loco essent res nostrae."[22] The core idea of the modern formula gleams through this formulation but there seems to be some confusion about the identity of the person responsible. On one hand, Nelson believes Melderius is a pseudonym for Petrus Meiderlin, a Lutheran theologian from Augsburg.[23] On the other hand, Blanford, on whom Nelson seemed to have somewhat relied, refers to Rupertus Melderius as a "Dutch leader."[24]

Although there is use of the formula in the Reformation period, we do not have enough evidence to link its origin to that period. The most that can be said with certainty is that its use can be traced back to that period but, as we have seen, a version of the formula predated the Reformation. Although Nelson does not deal with the pre-reformation era, he does not seem to allow for an earlier tradition.

When we look carefully at the writings of Lukas of Prague (d. 1528), who spans the period from pre-Reformation to Reformation, one gets the impression of a continuity of the idea behind the formula in Moravian thought. Luke of Prague was the leading theologian of the Moravian Church at the onset of the Lutheran Reformation. He made a distinction between things necessary/essential and non-essential things, which appears to be based on the old Moravian three-tiered doctrinal system. He insisted that the basic content and focus of faith was God's saving action: "therefore the essential things cannot be within the power of the people, the church or sacraments."[25] Lukas represents a resurrection of the legacy of John Hus, the Bohemiam Reformer, and has had a lasting effect on Moravian theology. Lukas of Prague is said to have reproached Luther in 1523 and Zwingli in 1527 for the one-sidedness in their understanding of the gospel and remained virtually unaffected by their work.[26] His theological position was under-girded by the principle of "the distinguishing of those things which are essential and those things which are merely helpful for salvation."[27] It may be, then, that in Lukas of Prague we find a link between the three-tiered doctrinal systems that we referred to in the previous section and the two-tiered distinction between "essentials" and "non-essentials" that seemed to have become more dominant in the period of the Reformation.

After 1567, the relationship between the Moravians and the Lutherans became strained, which, according to Rican, was due to Luther's' concern about their theology, "that is, their teaching on essential and helpful things."[28] However, McNeill's view that "unresolved differences" were related to the Moravians holding to seven sacraments, and their practices of celibacy and rebaptism, seems to point to the more likely cause of the conflict.[29] The Consensus of Sendomir, a mutual agreement between the Unitas Fratrum, the Reformed and the Lutheran churches in Poland in 1570, seems to reflect the spirit of the formula, in as much as it "was primarily a pledge of mutual forbearance and charity."[30] It declared that all the parties would avoid dissension while striving to maintain peace and tranquillity; things that were necessary for the building up of the church.[31] Johannes Plitt is probably right in linking the formula with this agreement[32] although, as we have seen, it obviously reflects an approach held at least by the Moravians quite some time before the signing of that Consensus.

Since the Reformation, the distinction between necessary and non-necessary things has become an important instrument of forging unity between different doctrinal positions. McNeill underlines this by noting that the idea of 'fundamental articles' recurred with great frequency in the 17th century discussions of union.[33] This is further verified by the many personalities of the Reformation in whose writings we see various allusions to the formula. First among them is John Calvin, who held the view that diversity on non-essential matters ought not to be an occasion for disunity.[34] He cites as essential points of doctrine that, God is one, that Christ is God and the Son of God, and that our salvation lies in God's mercy.[35] Similarly Cassander, a Flemish scholar of the Erasmian school, made proposals for unity based on a demarcation of the essentials in doctrine.[36] Like Calvin, Bucer, and Cranmer, Erasmus had distinguished essential from non-essential beliefs in relation to the problem of unity and separation.[37] Martin Schmidt mentions another writer of the Erasmian School, Acontius (d. 1566) who also formulated the idea that a distinction should be made between articles of the faith that are necessary to salvation, and those that are of secondary importance.[38] Thus a long line of Christian Humanists extending from Erasmus (1467–1536)[39] to Johannes Hulsemann (1602–1661) worked with the central thought of identifying a minimum of Christian dogma that was necessary to salvation.[40]

COMENIUS AND THE BOHEMIAN FORMULA

The Erasmian/humanist tradition and the work of the Reformers who desired a unity on the basis of fundamental things necessary for salvation form the background of the work of John Amos Comenius (1592–1670). He was bishop of the Moravian Church (Unitas Fratrum) from 1648 to his death in 1670. As the most outstanding leader of the church in the seventeenth century, he is known for his irenic work as well as his educational reforms. Comenius' thinking shaped much of the later tradition of the Unitas Fratrum that merged with the Lutherans and Reformed strands to form the renewed Moravian church in 1727. In his work entitled *Unum Necessarium* (One Thing Necessary) published in 1668, he said that the prime law of the Christian concord is threefold: to maintain unity in necessary things, freedom in less necessary things, (which they call diaphora) and love in all things.[41] This formulation is very close to the way it is preserved in the Moravian Church today, which explains the tendency of Moravians to credit Comenius with the original wording. Comenius has no doubt significantly influenced the modern Moravian usage of the formula and he may be another link between the modern formula and the earlier Moravian distinction between "essentials," "auxiliary" and "incidental." It is noteworthy that this original distinction was not formally made in the confessions of the Unity after 1535.[42] However, for Comenius, the legacy of the Unitas Fratrum, which speaks of faith in Christ as king, was built on the doctrine of the essential and ministrative things of Christianity.[43] Comenius has served the whole Christian enterprise well by giving a new impetus to the use of the formula. In doing so, however, he was only building on a tradition within his own church as well as that of a line of Christian thinkers that preceded him with similar interest in unity.

The inclination to seek unity on the basis of necessary things, which became widespread in the seventeenth century discourse, makes it doubtful that the formula came into usage in Britain by way of Baxter, as Nelson suggests.[44] It is felt that the motto of that famous Englishman was: in necessary things, unity; in doubtful things, liberty; in all things, charity.[45] The third part of the formula, "in all things charity" may indeed be a later addition, but the evidence suggests that the theologian or humanist, who in the seventeenth century subscribed to this motto, was standing in a long tradition of more than one hundred years. It is evident that by the time of Comenius, a contemporary of Baxter, there were more consistent occurrences of the same wording of the formulation as is found in current usage. The death of Comenius in 1670 marks a turning point in the history of the Unitas Fratrum and its attempts at healing the divisions of the Reformation. With his passing we then turn to the Post-Reformation period.

Daniel Ernst Jablonski (1660–1741), Bishop of the Moravian Church from 1699–1741, followed in Comenius' footsteps in the use of the formula. Jablonski studied at Oxford (1680–1683) where he met and was friendly with William Wake who later became Archbishop of Canterbury.[46] With Wake he shared the idea that fundamentals of the faith should be distinguished from the non-fundamentals.[47] Wake considered that latitude and flexibility should be given and differences should be allowed on secondary issues, for example, issues such as the doctrines of the Eucharist, predestination and election.[48] The friendship between Wake and Jablonski from university days is reflected in the correspondence between them during the early years of the eighteenth century, during which Jablonski sought to establish an Anglican pattern of episcopacy in the Church in Prussia.[49] Applying the principle of the formula, Jablonski sought to achieve organic union between the churches on the basis of agreement on fundamentals of the Christian faith and an agreement to differ on non-fundamentals, rites and ceremonies.[50] Thus, the friendly waters of inter-church ecumenism, which was rising in the seventeenth and eighteenth centuries, nurtured what had become known as an ideal, which was held in particular Christian community for centuries.

THE POST-REFORMATION PERIOD

It would seem that there is a correlation between the renewal of the Moravian Church and use of the Bohemian Formula in its present form. The Moravian Church was virtually wiped out in Bohemia and Moravia by the second half of the seventeenth century. Some members were exiled; some were persecuted, while others emigrated particularly to Poland and Germany.[51] In the foreign lands they returned to the Roman Catholic Church or became members of Lutheran or Reformed Churches. The renewal of the Moravian Church in Germany was made possible through a number of migrant families that expressed a certain fidelity to the traditions of the old Unitas Fratrum. These individuals were given a place to settle on the estate belonging to Count Zinzendorf in Hennesdorf.[52]

With the renewal of the Church under the leadership of Zinzendorf (1700–1760), its doctrinal emphases reflected the ideals of Lutheran pietism and priority to world mission, to which Zinzendorf was entirely committed. Hamilton notes that, the theology of the Brethren's Church in the Zinzendorfian era was completely identified with the theology of Zinzendorf.[53] He held a radical christocentric approach to theology, which served as a unifying ideal for the Lutheran, Reformed and Brethren ways (*Trophen*) of apprehending saving truth,[54] which were recognised within the Moravian Unity. During the time of Zinzendorf we do not hear much of the distinction between the essentials and the non-essentials, as much as we hear of the need to apprehend the one thing needful for salvation.[55] Zinzendorf's Lutheran background gave him a preference for the Augsburg Confession, even though the language of "the essentials" is not missing from his work. For example, on September 25, 1746 he gave a sermon in London entitled "On the Essential Character and Circumstances of the Life of a Christian," the purpose of which was to make clear what constitutes the essential Christian.[56] However, as of 1775 the pre-eminence of the Lutheran heritage expressed in the Augsburg Confession was de-emphasized. While postulating five essentials, the Synod adhered to the principle of liberality in non-essentials, refusing to arbitrarily bind the conscience of all members by the formulation of a detailed creed.[57] This refusal to insist on a particular creed would become significant in the later years of Moravian Church History. Today Moravians affirm several of the historic creeds but they see creeds as human statements that will never be able to capture in totality the mystery to which they allude.

The old Bohemian formula resurfaced in the immediate post-Zinzendorfian era, having been preserved by those who constituted the renewed church. This took place at the Synod at Barby in 1775, fifteen years after the death of Zinzendorf. By the resurrection of the old distinction between essentials and non-essentials,[58] the Moravian Unity retrieved and re-emphasised what had been a lost aspect of its self-understanding. The change of discourse to reflect the older tradition was a critical development in the life of the Moravian Church. This articulation of the Church's self-understanding was not merely theoretical, but a concrete description of the reality derived from the Lutheran, Reformed and Moravian strands (*Trophen*). The *Church Book of the Brethren's Unity* published in London 1892 asserts:

> The cordial connection founded on the essential oneness that subsists between the Renewed Brethren's Church and the whole Protestant Church, and which within our own Church pale cemented the descendants of the Ancient Brethren's Church and those from the 'Lutheran' and 'Reformed' Churches joined us, as one Brethren's Unity, was more accurately explained at our Synod in the year 1744 . . . 'the Renewed Brethren's Church recognizes within herself three 'Troposes.'[59]

The Synod of 1879, the report of which was carried in the *Church Book* of 1892 read the decision of the Synod of 1744 as refashioning the idea of unity in essentials, which was descriptive of a theological position, into a statement of ecclesiology, that is, of how the church was to be understood. Consequently, Bishop Hasse in a 1907 sermon at Fetter Lane on the 450th Anniversary of the Church said, "our Church's motto has long been: 'in essentials, Unity; in non-essentials, Liberty; in all things, Charity'."[60] In the period after 1879 it became difficult to speak about Moravian theology without at the same time referring to the Bohemian Formula. One sees the dynamic relationship between the way the Moravians understood the nature of the church and the theology in the 1892 *Church Book*, which states that:

> We aim at the comprehension, in a higher living unity, of the diversity of doctrinal views, in so far as this diversity turns on the interpretation of Scripture, and

arises from the different modes in which the same scriptural truth is apprehended by different minds. This aim however, we do not seek to attain by simply shutting the door on differences of opinion, or by leaving them unnoticed. . . . We seek rather a positive living unity. This we find in the faith in the crucified Christ, in whom as in the Son of God, we have reconciliation unto God. . . . He that knows he is one with us in these points is heartily welcomed with the right hand of brotherly fellowship. . . . And we do this not only within our membership, but we seek also to let it be known and felt towards those without.[61]

There was the recognition that even within a given congregation or communion different ways of interpreting Scripture would emerge. The challenge was to find a unity in the faith that rose above the different interpretations. This is a challenge that interpreters of the Bible and the Qur'an continue to face. When a given mode of interpretation becomes crystallized into a sort of creed it robs the community of the richness of the diversity and consigns future generations to rubber-stamping their interpretation. Delineating the essentials in the faith was therefore seen as a way of getting around the difficulties of interpretation. The Book of Order of 1911 sees the formula as the thread that joins the old Unitas Fratrum to the new. It states: "As the oldest in the sisterhood of Protestant Churches, she [the Moravian Church] stands today as in the beginning, for unity in essentials, for liberty in non-essentials, for love in all things. 'In necessariis unitas, in non necessariis libertas, in omnibus caritas.'"[62]

The simplicity and clarity of stating essentials, however, proved extremely vulnerable to the theological ferment especially in Germany around 1900. This theological ferment showed that the limits to diversity could be breached even within the Moravian Church. Of particular concern to the Brethren was "the thought of Albrecht Ritschl, which sought to frame a new apologetic synthesis between the Christian faith and the new knowledge.[63] Though the General Synod of 1909 reaffirmed the principles of that of 1879, the tensions at the Synod indicated that a new dispensation in Moravian theology was dawning. However, it was not until the Synod of 1957 that the new dispensation was officially ushered in. Rather than detailing the essentials in doctrine, as was customary, the Synod approved what was called the "Ground of Unity,"[64] effectively shifting the emphasis from clarity in theological fundamentals to mission, as the vocation of the church. The Church was understood as an instrument of God's kingdom and the specificity of doctrines was further de-emphasized. For example, the "Ground of Unity" asserts that:

The Unitas Fratrum is, therefore, aware of its being called to serve mankind. . . . With the whole of Christendom we share faith in God the Father, the Son, and the Holy Spirit. . . . We recognize ourselves to be a church of sinners. . . . The Unitas

Fratrum realizes that the mystery of Jesus Christ to which the Bible bears witness cannot be fully comprehended in any human statement. . . . The Unitas Fratrum recognizes in the creeds of the Church the thankful acclaim of the Body of Christ.[65]

This vocational emphasis in the understanding of the church took the place of the reference to specific doctrines. Despite the approval of the "Ground of Unity," which for the rank and file of the church may be very nebulous, the formula "in essentials unity, in non-essentials liberty, in all things charity," is still treated as a succinct description of what it is to be Moravian. As the history of the formula shows, between 1775 and 1957, distinguishing "essentials" from "non-essentials" was an important theological task for the Unity. The Bohemian Formula should then be treated as a classical description of Moravian understanding. Therefore any use that is made of it in theological discourse today should refer to its subsistence in the Moravian Church.

The Bohemian formula then, has served the Moravian Church both in terms of its internal and external relations. It may well be an indispensable basis for inter-church and interfaith relations. Early attempts at unity in the ecumenical movement drew on the formula. Now the challenge is to apply the same formula to the way Christians relate to Islam.

The historical survey of the formula, "in essentials unity, in non-essentials liberty, in all things charity," shows its usefulness for dealing with issues of Christian unity and co-operation. However, some people may find it quite a leap to jump with it from an inter-church situation to deal with an inter-faith situation because the Church and another religious faith are not based on the same assumption. In fact, for some people, Christianity and Islam are based on first principles that contradict each other: Christianity will not compromise the centrality of Jesus as witnessed in Holy Scripture and Islam will not compromise the centrality of the Qur'an and the role of the Prophet Muhammad. It would seem then that such an attempt runs into difficulties of methodology. Can one, therefore, justify making this leap to attempt to apply this notion of "essentials" to the relationship between Christianity and Islam? In what follows, it will be argued that despite its difficulties, the notion of "essentials" can justifiably be used in coming to a theological position on Islam as well as in helping to clarify what Christians can truly say of the Muslin faith.

TOWARDS AN INTERFAITH FORMULA

While the Moravian Unity was moving to substitute the idea of a hierarchy in doctrines, as expressed the in Bohemian Formula, for a more general statement of ecclesiology, the idea was resurfacing as a leading concept in ecumenism.

In the Second Vatican Council Pope John, Cardinal Bea, and others drew to the attention of the Roman Catholic Church the important distinction between the unchanging deposit of the faith and the changing, changeable manner, mode, language etc., in which it is presented.[66] Alluding to the idea of the Bohemian formula, the Decree on Ecumenism calls attention to unity, liberty and charity with respect to doctrine: while preserving unity in essentials, all members of the church, according to the office entrusted to each, should preserve freedom in the variety of liturgical rites, and even in the theological elaborations of revealed truth; and that in all things charity be exercised.[67] This distinction between the essentials of the faith and the elaborations of the revealed truth, in which there is variety (in consequence of which there must be freedom), was further developed and applied to the relationship between Catholics and "separated brethren." The section of the Decree dealing with the practice of Ecumenism asserts that Catholic theologians engaged in ecumenical dialogue, while standing fast by the teaching of the Church and searching together with separated brethren into the divine mysteries, should act with love for truth, with charity and with humility. When comparing doctrines, they should remember that in Catholic teaching there exists an order or 'hierarchy' of truths, since they vary in their relationship to the foundation of the Christian faith.[68] This idea of truths organized around the centre or foundation of the faith is reminiscent of the distinction between "essentials," "auxiliary" and "accidentals," which was made by the early Bohemian Brethren. It is also reminiscent of the Reformation period in which churches summarized the truths of the faith in catechisms meant for the edification of the people of God.[69]

The conclusion of the Joint Working Group of the World Council of Churches and the Roman Catholic Church alludes to the need to go in the direction of the Bohemian formula. The Working Group argued that a 'hierarchy of truths' may also be a means of ensuring that the necessary expressions of the faith in various cultures do not result in any loss of its content or in a separation of the Christian truths from the foundation.[70] In other words, the formula, which preserves the notion of a hierarchy of truths, may be a useful means for addressing different expressions of faith in different cultures. It is this idea of using the notion of hierarchy of truths in different cultures that gives the formula, "in essentials unity, in non-essentials liberty, in all things charity," its interfaith applicability.

The religiously plural culture in which we live challenges Christians to take account of people of other faiths, in a way that does not lead to Christian truths being dislodged from their foundation. A major fear that we have among Christians is that to talk to people of other faiths on equal terms may result in the diluting of the distinctiveness of Christian truths. However, the formula preserves the notion of hierarchy of truths, which is necessary in context where different emphases are held, even within the same communion. Maintaining a hierarchy of truths is an approach that Christians in general can affirm. The Bohemian formula, therefore, may be the most viable basis on which to construct an approach to interfaith dialogue today. This dialogue, we must hasten to add is no longer an option in a plural context. Even if it does not happen formally, it is still a necessary way we have to approach people of other faiths. The minute we dismiss the significance of the faiths, to which people commit their lives in all sincerity, it becomes a dismissal of the significance of the adherents themselves. The choices they make have to be respected even when we do not agree with them.

The Second Vatican Council in its Declaration of the Relationship of the Church to Non-Christian Religions seemed to have had in mind such a basis as the Bohemian formula implies. In declaring that the Church looks upon the Muslims with esteem the Declaration mentions what can be said of Islam. The Muslims, it declares: "adore one God, . . . they revere Him [Jesus] as a prophet. They also honour Mary . . . they await the day of judgement . . . they prize the moral life, and give worship to God especially through prayer, almsgiving, and fasting."[71] In commenting on the Declaration, Anawati notes that it gives an account of the Muslim understating of the rule of God in the human affairs in the shortest possible form, but not of the essence of the Muslim faith, which is summed up, for example, in the *Shahadah*.[72] The *Shahadah* states that there is no God but God and Muhammad is his prophet. This accounting for the faith of Muslims from the standpoint of those things considered fundamental in Christianity was the starting point of the openness towards people of other faiths for which Vatican II has become known. Likewise, the formula holds for Christians in general the prospect of moving from exclusivity towards openness and inclusivity. Inclusivity is not merely a willingness to let every idea and practice exist. Instead, it is directed toward specific objectives such as freeing humankind from injustice and servitude to other human beings so that they may be free to worship God.[73] In other words, being inclusive is not about surrendering one's faith. Rather, it is making issues of justice to take pre-eminence over issues of doctrine, which in effect means insisting on a certain ethical ideal. Many Christians and Muslims can only speak with confidence about their faith in stating that it is the only true faith, to which all else must be subordinated. Such an approach between the two religions is no longer viable. By starting with the Bohemian formula, the way is opened for a new approach, which must not be seen as a final step but rather as a necessary first step.

The notion of "essentials," as it will be used in this study, then, is not about giving an essence of the religion. Rather, it is an attempt to give an account of Christianity and Islam, in terms of things fundamental to their respective self-understanding. The Muslim-Christian Research Groups notes that when believers in one religion seek to understand the faith of believers of another religion, "they must go back to the terms of their own faith."[74] In the next two chapters, we shall, therefore, consider some things that are fundamental to both Christian and Muslim self-understanding.

NOTES

1. A. Schultze, *Christian Doctrine and Systematic Theology* (Bethlehem, PA: Moravian Church College, 1914), iv. In the 1979 reprinting, the editors noted that this publication had been for more that half-a-century the most definitive statement of the theology of the Moravian Church in English. The formula is used also in several publications meant for popular reading. For example, it is seen in *The Moravian*, a monthly publication of the Provinces of the Moravian Church in North America, as well as on several Internet websites of Moravian Churches.

2. Made by Vernon Nelson, Moravian Archivist in Bethlehem Pennsylvania, in an undated and unpublished article. The article, entitled "The Slogan, 'in essentials unity, in non-essentials liberty, in all things charity' " is in Moravian Archives in Bethlehem and a copy is in this writer's possession.

3. J. H. Blanford, "In Essentials, Unity; in Non-Essentials, Liberty; in All Things, Charity" *The Moravian Messenger*, Vol. XL No. II (November 1930), 125.

4. Blanford, "In Essentials," 125

5. In R. Rouse, et al, Eds., *A History of the Ecumenical Movement 1517–1968* (Geneva: WCC Publications, 1993), 19. My emphasis.

6. According to Schweinitz, this document was found in a Lissa Folio. See E. De Schweinitz, *The History of the Church Known as The Unitas Fratrum or the Unity of the Brethren* (Bethlehem, PA: The Moravian Publication Concern, 1901), 200, note 1.

7. Schweinitz, *The History of the Church*, 201.

8. Schweinitz, *History,* 201. Schweinitz has "*accidentilia*" which seems to be an error.

9. Rudolf Rican, *The History of the Unity of the Brethren: A Protestant Hussite Church in Bohemia and Moravia,* trans. by D. Crews (Bethlehem, PA: Moravian Church in America, 1992), 403. Kalich first published this book in Prague in 1957.

10. Schweinitz, *History,* 406. It is believed that this catechism is based on an earlier version published in 1505 that is now lost, which is also traceable to John Hus. See Schweinitz, *History*, 407 note 2.

11. E. de Schweinitz, *The Catechism of the Bohemian Brethren*, (Bethlehem, PA: Moravian Publication Office, 1869), 6.

12. Schweinitz, *The Catechism*, 14.

13. *De Trinitate*, V, ii, 3 in 1977 edition of E. Przywara, *An Augustine Synthesis* (London: Sheed and Ward, 1936), 98. Emphases mine.

14. *Epistolae* CXX, ii, 8, Przywara, Augustine, 60.

15. *De Trinitate libri quindecim* VIII, iv,.6; ix, 13 in E. Przywara, 61.

16. *Sermones* CCIX in Przywara, 234.

17. See W. R. Estep, *Renaissance & Reformation* (Grand Rapids, Michigan: Eerdmans, 1986), 65 & 73. Estep argues that Wycliffe borrowed the concepts of the church as "triumphant" "militant" and "sleeping" from Augustine.

18. Przywara, v.

19. Rican, *History of the Unity*, 404.

20. Rican, 404.

21. V. Nelson, "The Slogan," 1.

22. Nelson, 3.

23. Nelson, 3.

24. Blanford, "In Essentials," 1.

25. Rican, 393.

26. Rican, 393.

27. Rican, 393.

28. Rican, 396.

29. Rouse, 42.

30. Rouse, 62.

31. Rouse, 63.

32. Nelson, 2.

33. J. T. McNeill, "The Ecumenical Idea and Efforts to Realize it, 1517–1618," in Rouse, 38.

34. Rouse, 32.

35. Rouse, 38.

36. Rouse, 38.

37. Rouse, 38.

38. M. Schmidt, "Ecumenical Activity on the Continent of Europe in the Seventeenth and Eighteenth Centuries," Rouse, 75.

39. Some traditions refer to 1466 and 1469 as dates of birth. See Estep, 78–79.

40. Rouse, 79.

41. Nelson, 4. See also Nelson, "A translation of John Amos Comenius' *Unum Necessarium*," a thesis presented to Moravian Theological College Bethlehem, Pennsylvania, 1958.

42. Rican, 406.

43. Rican, 400.

44. Nelson, 5.

45. Nelson, 5.

46. Rouse, 154.

47. Rouse, 154.

48. Rouse, 155.

49. Rouse, 153.

50. Rouse 153.

51. J. Hamilton, *A History of the Church Known as the Moravian Church or Unitas Fratrum or Unity of the Brethren: during the eighteenth and nineteenth centuries* (Bethlehem, PA: Times Publishing Company, 1900), 6.

52. Hamilton, *A History of the Church*, 8. Hamilton notes that the Synod of 1756 records that there were 1014 members living of Moravian parentage, 629 of whom were born in Bohemia. Zinzendorf also recorded at the same Synod that 38 brothers

and 45 sisters had died after serving in the ministry at home or on the mission field. See Hamilton, 9.

53. Hamilton, 189.

54. Hamilton, 193.

55. Hamilton, 193.

56. G. Forell, Ed., *Nicholas Ludwig Count von Zinzendorf, Bishop of the Church of the Moravian Brethren: Nine Public Lectures on Important Subjects in Religion: Preached in Fetter Lane Chapel in London in the year 1746* (Iowa City: University of Iowa Press, 1973), 75ff. Zinzendorf describes the relationship between the believer and Christ in terms of a marriage in which one partner took the name of the other to indicate belonging.

57. Hamilton, 220.

58. Hamilton, 220.

59. *The Church Book of the Brethren's Unity in the British Province* (London: Moravian Publication Office, 1892) p. 12

60. Hasse, "Consider the Days of Old," *Moravian Messenger* Vol. XVIII (1908) 76.

61. *The Church Book of the Brethren's Unity*, 9.

62. *Book of Order of the Moravian Church* (Bethlehem, PA: The Provincial Elders' Conference, 1911), 4.

63. C. D. Crews, *Confessing Our Unity in Christ: Historical and Theological Background to "The Ground of Unity"* (Winston Salem, NC: Moravian Archives, 1994), 15.

64. Crews, *Confessing our Unity*, 26.

65. Section of the 1957 "Ground of Unity," *Manual of the Moravian Church in Jamaica*, 1990, 2.

66. W. M. Abbott, *The Documents of Vatican II* (USA: American Press, 1966) 349, note 27

67. Abbott, *The Documents of Vatican II*, 349

68. Abbott, 354.

69. Joint Working Group WCC/RC, "The 'Notion of Hierarchy of Truths'— An Ecumenical Interpretation" *One in Christ* Vol. XXVII No. 3 (1991): 287.

70. Joint Working Group, "Hierarchy of Truths," 292.

71. Abbott, 663.

72. G. Anawati, "Excursus on Islam" in H. Vorgrimler, Ed., *Commentary on the Documents of Vatican II: Volume III* (New York: Herder and Herder, 1969) p. 153: Anawati notes that some reproached the Declaration for being too minimalist, while others reproached it for its silence on certain features of Muslim morality. (See Anawati, "Excursus," 152.)

73. Esack, "Mulims Engaging the Other,"141.

74. S. Brown, *The Challenge of the Scriptures*, 88.

Chapter Three

The Essentials in Islam

FAITH AND PRAXIS

The formula, "in essentials unity, in non-essential liberty, in all things charity," of which we have been speaking, has generally been used in a Christian context. If we seek to use this formula in a non-Christian context we are immediately faced with some difficulties. For example, if we use it in Islam, we are faced with the difficulties associated with trying to give a universally acceptable definition of what may be called essential doctrines of Islam. One difficulty is that Muslims are more concerned with right conduct or orthopraxis than with right belief (orthodoxy).[1] Since conduct takes precedence over belief, it means that conduct is the criterion by which the doctrine is judged. This is somewhat different from the situation in Christianity where there has been a long tradition that insists on right belief. The doctrinal controversies in Christianity, going back to the fourth century, were largely about right beliefs. It is the emphasis on correct doctrinal formulations that gave rise to the Nicene Creed of the ecumenical councils, Luther's Longer Cathechism, the Thirty-Nine Articles of the Church of England, the Heidelberg Cathechism, and so on. These creeds were (and in some cases still are) treated as confessions to which those who held the truth as defined by the particular community had to subscribe. One can say that the whole Protestant movement itself was largely constructed around the correctness of confessional statements, as the basis of a church's identity. For this reason, the creeds of Christianity are important lines of demarcations for those believed to be on the right path and those considered not being on the right path. In more recent times, sections within the Christian community have been finding that subscribing to certain doctrinal formulations are not sufficient to demarcate the true Christian. For example, Paul Knitter argues that as liberation theology has shown that we cannot begin to know Jesus unless we are following him, so also it can clarify the conditions for the possibility of claiming any kind of uniqueness or exclusiveness for Jesus. Such uniqueness and exclusiveness "can be known and then affirmed only 'in its concrete embodiment,' only in the praxis of historical involvement."[2] Zinzendorf of the Moravian community made a similar allusion to the limitation of giving verbal assent to doctrine when he said that the *fiducia implicita*[3] (i.e. implicit faith), as expressed in the thief on the cross, was more important than subscribing to doctrinal statements. In fact, he explicitly rejects the practice whereby communities and individuals were declared Christians because they made assent to a given statement of faith.

When we consider Islam, however, there would not be a doctrinal belief in Islam that would be equivalent to the Christian doctrine of justification by faith, which some Lutherans and Roman Catholics call the mother of all doctrines. Furthermore, even though there have been attempts to formulate credal statements in Islam, that faith community has nothing that would be analogous to the Nicene Creed or the Apostles' Creed. So when it comes to the idea of essential doctrines, the situation in Islam is somewhat different from that which we find in Christianity. Farid Esack asserts that the Qur'an is a book of understanding through praxis, rather than one of doctrine and dogma.[4] It is not so much about belief as much as it is about how to live.

Another difficulty we face in speaking of essentials in Islam is that there is no precise equivalence in the Arabic language for the word "orthodoxy" or "right teaching."[5] Islam is considered as a way of life, an interpretative framework (*gestalt*) in which everything is interconnected.[6] It is therefore contrary to the spirit of the faith to consider one aspect in isolation from the rest. Naturally, Christians will respond and say that in Christianity practice is as important as belief. However, Christians are agreed that while practice is important they are saved through believing, not through practice.

The emphasis on practice in Islam, though, does not mean that that faith community is not concerned with beliefs or a belief system. In fact, one can locate different philosophical and juridical traditions in today's Islam, which result in different emphases in the interpretation of the Qur'an and in the way different accounts of the history of the religion are presented.[7] It is for this reason that we find wide variations of conduct, with some groups claiming that others are not being true to the faith of Islam. Consequently, though the term "essentials" may be more akin to Christian discourse, one may still speak of fundamentals of the faith that Muslims in general would regard as being non-negotiable.

The faithful in Islam and Christianity can appreciate the spirit of the Bohemian formula because it can find application in faith communities. When we look at literature on Islam, that is written by both Muslims and non-Muslims, we see an attempt to indicate those aspects of the faith that are considered fundamental. For example, David Shenk has listed five pillars of belief on which he says Muslims agree.[8] These are (1) Belief in one God only (2) Belief in the prophets of God (3) Belief in the Books of God (4) Belief in angels (5) Belief in the final judgement. A. H. Muhmud, himself a Muslim, says there are three things that belong to the essence of Islam: (1) confessing the *Shahadah*, (2) believing everything that Muhammad proclaimed, and (3) practising all that Islam enjoins and refraining from what it forbids.[9] Ann-Marie Schimmel says a Muslim is a person who pronounces the *Shahadah* and accepts the validity of the *Shari' a* as the God-given path on which to walk.[10] Andrew Rippin believes that the inscription on the Dome of the Rock in Jerusalem indicates Muslim self-understanding at the time of the capture of Jerusalem, a self-understanding that has survived until today. It says: "Muslims [are] those who believe in God, what He revealed to Muhammad, and that there is no difference among the prophets, all of whom God sent."[11] The differences in these accounts of "essentials" are evident, but they do give a justification for using the term "essentials" in respect of the Muslim faith. If one were to distil a single list of three things from the items listed above, one could regard these as the things on which Muslims most certainly agree as being fundamental to the practice of their faith. The three things are: (a) the oneness of God, (a) the Qur'an as God's final speech and (c) the exemplary role of the Prophet Muhammad. Given the charges being made against Islam today and given the claims that are being made in the name of Islam, it will be important to explore these fundamental issues. The assertions people make must then be judged by their consistency with these fundamentals.

THE ONENESS (UNICITY) OF GOD

The non-negotiable belief that there is only one God is of fundamental importance in Islam. It is also a belief central to Christianity and Judaism, which together with Islam are referred to as the three Abrahamic faiths. It is to be noted that the emergence of Islam as a distinct religion was characterized by the affirmation that there is no deity but God. This insistence on the oneness of God had an earth-shaking effect on the context in which Islam emerged, a context which, among other things, was known for its polytheism. Muslims preserve the affirmation that there is no god but God in what they call the *Shahadah*. In Arabic it runs as follows: "*la ilaha illa Llah Alla.*" The fact that the saying is repeated again and again in the Qur'an is testimony to its importance and centrality. The oneness of God is at the core of the *adham*, that is, the call that is sounded from the minaret, which summons the faithful to gather for worship on Fridays. The *adham* declares:

> God is most great. God is most great. I bear witness that there is no god except God. I bear witness that Muhammad is the Apostle of God. Come to prayer. Come unto good. Prayer is better than sleep. Come ye to the best deed. God is most great. God is most great. There is no god except God.[12]

The allusions and direct references to the oneness of God in pivotal events of the Qur'an further demonstrate the centrality and significance of the affirmation. One of those events is the set of revelations in Surah 112, which relate to the struggle against idolatry. According to the Qur'an, Allah, the only one deserving of worship, is eternal and absolute. God is not begotten and does not beget; there is none like God.[13] Muslims regard these revelations as being the most sublime in declaring the attributes of Allah. In order to get a fair idea of God we have to appreciate God's oneness. We should not think, though, that we have thereby fully grasped whom God in God's fullness for God remains beyond our imaginations. No creature, of whatever sort, can rival God for the worship that is truly due to God. Islam is an Abrahamic religion in which "Muhammad called his people away from idolatry."[14] Therefore, the imputation of idolatry to Islam has no foundation in the truth. Similarly, the idea that Islam is constructed on a commitment to violence was formulated during an era of even greater anti-Islamic rhetoric that there is today. Only the uneducated and uninformed will continue to hold such beliefs today.

When Christians consider the centrality of Jesus Christ for their faith, they are inclined to make a sharp line of demarcation between Christianity, on one hand and Judaism and Islam on the other. However, from a theological point of view, such a demarcation may not be justifiable. All three communities of faith affirm belief in one God, who is eternal, the creator. Ironically, some people in Judaism and Islam see Christianity as faltering on the question of God's oneness and unicity because of the doctrine of the Trinity. This, as we shall see, however, is based on a faulty understanding of that doctrine. The faithful in the three religions should consider more closely the designation made by Ovey Muhammed. According to this writer, the designation "Judeo-Christian tradition should be changed to the Judeo-Christian-Islamic tradition."[15] This assertion finds support with William Watt who has written extensively on Islam. According to Watt, despite contentions that different concepts of God obtain in Judaism, Christianity and Islam, they all affirm belief in the one God who is the God of Abraham.[16]

Although it is apparent to Christian and Jewish scholars that the strong monotheistic emphasis in Islam is directly linked to the Judo-Christian tradition, it is not so apparent to Muslim scholars. In fact, some Muslim scholars are inclined to deny that the rise of monotheism has anything to do with Judaeo-Christian/biblical roots. For example, Henninger has argued that the recognition of the creator as Allah predated Islam. Although this belief was not widespread, it was present at Mecca before the formal rise of Islam.[17] Josef van Ess takes the view that monotheism was a natural development in Mecca. According to him, the polytheism of Mecca could not cope with the problems posed by a bustling city trade, "because it was bound up with the tribal system through the local cults."[18] Allah, an Arabic word with a long ancestry, which seemed to have referred to the supreme or high God, came to be understood as reference to the only God. From an socio-economic point of view, it seems that the influence of the tribe that affirmed belief in Allah, whom they called the high God, became the dominant tribe. This reminds us of the classical Greek period, where the heavenly deities corresponded to the social stratification and the tensions between the different classes in the society.

It is even more interesting to note that some scholars do not credit the Prophet Muhammad with fostering the development of monotheism in Islam. More scholars are leaning towards the view that "by the time of Muhammad, certain trends towards monotheism seemed to have already been emerging within Arabian religion."[19] Therefore, to link the rise of monotheism in Arabian religion simply to Muhammad may serve to dislodge Islam from its Arabic roots and to deny Islam its natural evolutionary development. "Neither for Muhammad and Islam . . . nor for Jesus and Christianity was there from the beginning any *creatio ex nihilio,*" (that is, creation out of nothing).[20]

There is a growing body of opinion, therefore, that monotheism was already well accepted in the social milieu in which Islam came into being. The crucial point, though, is that whether from the biblical roots or through the evolutionary process in Arabian religion, the monotheism with the accent as preached by the Prophet Muhammad seemed to have been radical in the literal sense of the word. It represented what today may be called a paradigmatic shift because it forced a reorganisation of the thinking of people in Mecca. The Islamicist, Kenneth Cragg, credits Muhammad with bringing about this shift. In Cragg' view:

> Only the rigorous consolidation of the instincts of worship into a single fear under a sole authority, dominating in mercy all the circumstances of ecology and economy . . . could suffice to awe and control the prodigalities of tribal conflict.[21]

The denial of the existence of the other deities served to undermine the traditional customs and power structure of the Quraish tribe to which Muhammad belonged and who were the guardians of the sacred Ka'bah in Mecca. By engineering this consolidation, Muhammad also threatened to make null and void the leadership of the other tribes. His journey out of Mecca, the *Hijrah,* was significant because it not only officially inaugurated the Islamic era, but it also signalled the end of the polytheistic practices in Mecca. Those who sided with Muhammad in his migration to Medina "were crossing their own Rubicon."[22] It was a radical step from polytheism to monotheism, as a consequence of the Prophet's message. The *shahadah* links both these issues together: the oneness of God and the role of the Prophet. As a whole it represents "complementary aspects of the one faith, inseparable one from the other."[23]

So, even though the influence of Judaism and Christianity in the formation of Islam and the formulation of its monotheistic emphasis may be denied, there was the reliance on developments that preceded them. The point of all this is that the recognition of the oneness of God was not some later theological development in Islam but was part and parcel of its emergence and self-understanding.

THE PROBLEM OF THE TRINITY

The mission of Muhammad, according to one scholar, was not so much to proclaim the existence of God, as much as it was to deny the existence of all lesser deities.[24] In other words, God's existence is self-evident and does not require proof. However, it may be necessary to make the case that other deities that people worship ought not to be equalled with God. This way of viewing the mission of Muhammad is similar to what we find in the first of the Ten Commandments in Exodus: "thou shall have not other God besides me." (Ex 20: 3) The proclamation of radical monotheism seemed to have had important consequences not only for the tribal religions of Mecca, but ironically, also for Christianity, which was mistakenly understood as making reference to multiple gods in the doctrine of the Trinity. The author of the well-written book, *Jesus in the Qur'an*, Geoffery Parrinder, takes the view that Muhammad had contacts with Christians in Northern Arabia and in Syria.[25] He is at pain to make this point because of the strong efforts by some Islamic scholars to deny any such links with Christianity in those early years. If Parrinder is right, as this writer believes he is, then those contacts may have coincided with a time when there was much dispute about Christian authority and teaching, such that there was uncertainty as to what was orthodox doctrine.[26] The fact that the Qur'an deals with beliefs that were apparently held by some Christians suggests that remnants of earlier disputes in Christianity, which had a bearing on the nature of Christ and how God was to be understood, may have survived well into the Muslim era. This is certainly the case with the dispute over the doctrine of the Trinity, a problematic issue that has persisted from the fourth century to the present time. Naturally, the doctrine of the Trinity is part of the difficulty in the relations between Christians and Muslims. The Qur'an addresses the Trinitarian idea directly:

> O People of the Book! Commit no excesses in your religion: nor say of Allah aught but the truth. Christ Jesus the son of Mary was (no more than) a Messenger of Allah, and His Word, which he bestowed on Mary, and a Spirit proceeding from Him: so believe in Allah and His Messengers. Say not 'Trinity': desist.[27]

The Christian doctrine of the Trinity, as understood by Muhammad, was regarded as being blasphemous. The Qur'an in Surah 5: 73 says, "they do blaspheme who say: Allah is one of three in a Trinity." Parrinder suggests that the idea of the Trinity may have been understood, as least by the early Muslims, to mean reference to God the Father, Jesus the Son and Mary the Virgin as Mother.[28] This was certainly an erroneous understanding of the doctrine, but that line of misunderstanding once drawn and canonized in the Qur'an, helped to ensure that the doctrine remained a stumblingblock in the relationship between the two faiths to the present day. Both Christianity and Islam affirm belief in one God, one through the doctrine of the Trinity and the other without relying on that Christian concept. Therefore, Muslims who criticise Christians for holding a belief in three gods, are not in fact attacking Christianity but are responding to "a Christian heresy and orthodox Christians would agree with [their] criticisms."[29]

From a Christian perspective, the dispute over the Trinity is really a problem of how we come to an understanding of God. This is a difficulty in the relationship between Christian communions as well as between Christians and Muslim. The Pietist, Zinzendorf, for example, argued that seeing Jesus as God is a second order task of faith and need not be set as an issue in interfaith discourse. In fact, Zinzendorf objects to discussing the issue of the Trinity in a mixed setting. In his view, "no doctrinal system calculated for a mixed religious body ought to turn upon the mystery of the Holy Trinity, much less make the very introduction of it."[30]

OVERCOMING DISPUTES CONCERNING THE TRINITY

The allusion to the Christian doctrine of the Trinity in the Islamic affirmation of the oneness of God (Surah 4:171; 5:73) draws into tension the issues of the nature of Jesus and the Christian doctrine of the incarnation. The doctrine of the incarnation is probably best illustrated in John 1:18: "the Word became flesh and dwelt among us." Christians understand this to mean that the one who appeared as Jesus of Nazareth pre-existed. The incarnation refers, then, to God's revelation in a human being. The doctrine of the Trinity is an outgrowth of the debates of the fourth and the fifth centuries about how the person of Jesus was to be understood. We there cannot avoid dealing with the nature person of Jesus when we raise the issue of the Trinity.

In response to the problem of the Trinity, the popular theologian, Hans Kung, argues that acceptance of the doctrine of the Trinity is not a criterion for being a Christian. In his view, being a Christian is not about the doctrine of the Trinity, but belief in the one and only God, the practical imitation of Christ and trusting the power of God's Spirit.[31] The problem with Kung's view, though, is that it does not address the real difficulty that there is in the different conceptions of the God that we find in the two religious communities; it simply dismisses one as a non-essential. The fact that the christological debates led to the development of the doctrine of the Trinity shows clearly that the doctrine of the Trinity is inextricably bound up with orthodox understanding of what it is to be a Christian. It may not be possible then to exclude the Christian doctrine of the Trinity from the fundamentals of the Christian faith.

The way Jesus is presented in the Qur'an precludes Muslims from having a Trinitarian doctrine. That presentation of Jesus (quranic christology, if you like), even with modern attempts at new interpretation of critical texts,[32] includes the denial of the death (and consequently the resurrection) of Jesus. This is a problem for the Qur'an because the death of Jesus is a death that "no serious historian doubts"[33] and a death that no Christian denies. In its allusion to the doctrine of the Trinity, the Qur'an (Surah 4:171) also explicitly denies the divinity of Christ. In other words, there is not only a rejection of the cross, which is central to the Christian faith; there is also a rejection of the way in which Christians account for the divine unity. Yet, when taken at face value, both Christians and Muslims hold a common belief in one God.

From the earliest days of the Islamic faith, it was perceived that the affirmation of the oneness of God was at variance with the understanding of God as Trinity. However, the idea of God as Trinity is related to Christian proclamation of Jesus of Nazareth. Part of the reason Muslims today are suspicious of the notion of God, as Trinity, is that the Qur'an itself has cast doubt on that notion. Our next task, then, is to look at the question of the status of the Qur'an, in which we have the denial of the Trinity alongside the proclamation of God's unicity.

THE QUR'AN AS GOD'S FINAL SPEECH

The eighteenth century theologian John Amos Comenius approached the problem of the dispute over the nature of God between Muslims and Christians from the point of view of what is revealed in sacred writings. In his view, we need to solve the basic problem of whether the Qur'an is of the same revelatory quality as the Bible. Can Christians regard the Qur'an as revelation from God as Muslims do? By formulating the issue in this way Comenius situates himself at the centre of today's theological debate. One Roman Catholic scholar, Dupuis, has argued that the fullness of revelation in Jesus, which we find in the Christian scriptures, does not gainsay the possibility of other scriptures being termed "word of God."[34] The difference between Comenius and Dupuis is that the latter allows for the possibility of Qur'an being called word of God but does not say on what basis. Comenius, on the other hand, goes further and is prepared to accept the Qur'an as revelatory, if it meets the basic of criteria he proposes for determining revelatory texts. In this way Comenius' approach is more intentionally dialogical, as a result of which his conclusion is more categorical. For Comenius, both the Bible and the Qur'an must be subjected to the same criteria for determining their revelatory quality. This is different from the attitude that we find in the contemporary debate. Comenius realised that the onus was also on the Christian to prove that their scriptures were also of a revelatory nature, since they had that expectation of Muslims. Being attuned to pluralism and committed to a process of public enquiry into truth, Comenius does not assume that the revelatory character of the Bible was clear to all. In order to establish this he proceeds by first seeking agreement on the fact that God speaks to us in our scriptures. How we understand God, then, is a question of the revelation that we have received, which has been recorded in Holy Scripture.

In the relationship between Christians and Muslims it is not recommended that any discussion begin with whether the doctrine of the Trinity can be established. The discussion should begin with whether Muslims regard the Bible as revelation from God. Christians must also clear their minds on the question of whether the Qur'an is revelation from God. This is an important issue, not only because Muslims regard the Qur'an as God's final speech but also because the Qur'an speaks about Jesus. Within the question of the status of the Qur'an we must also consider what it has to say about Jesus. The importance of this issue for the two faith communities cannot be overstated because Jesus is seen differently in the two religious communities. A closer observation of the Qur'an and how it speaks of Jesus may yield a better understanding of the foundations of the tension between the Muslim and Christian understanding of God. More importantly, only a genuine attempt to situate oneself in the worldview of one who sees the Qur'an as God's speech can one appreciate the role of the Qur'an in Muslim piety.

There is evidently no difficulty today for non-Muslims to affirm that the Qur'an is the sacred text for the Muslim faith. That does not mean, though, that non-Muslims will readily affirm unconditionally that the Qur'an is a divine word for all humanity. Indeed, the status of the Muslim Scriptures is a source of much contention between Muslims and people of other religions. For the Muslim faithful, the belief that the Qur'an is the divine word that came through the Prophet, as God's final speech, guarantees that the Qur'an has a most elevated position among the essentials of the Islamic faith. The meaning of the word Qur'an is to be found in the Arabic word *Iqra*, which we find at the beginning of Surah 96. The form *Iqra* is the active imperative singular of the root *qur'a,* from which the word Qur'an derives.[35] It may translate "read," "recite," or "proclaim aloud" (the last of these is used in Yasuf 'Ali's translation).

The self-understanding of the Muslim is connected to the Qur'an in a manner analogous to the way in which the self-understanding of the Christian is linked to the person of Jesus. The emergence of the Muslim community is intimately connected to the emergence of the Qur'an as a text that defines the limits and the character of its life. "The Koran is indeed the key to Muslims' *Weltanschauung* [worldview]."[36] However, the way in which the Qur'an functions in Islamic piety is somewhat different from the way in which the Bible functions, by and large, for Christians. For the ·Muslim, the Qur'an is "the *verbum visible*, the word inlibrate . . . which corresponds to the Word Incarnate of the Christian faith."[37] In van Ess's term, "the Qur'an is the word made book."[38] This norm of the Qur'an as God's uncreated word was achieved after a raging debate on the issue that took place within Islam in the early ninth century C.E. On one hand, there were the Hanbalites (named after ibn Hanbal 780–855)[39] who, together with the majority of the Muslim faithful, held that the Qur'an was uncreated. They argued that the revelation, which was given to Muhammad, was a copy of the heavenly book. On the other hand, there were the Mu'tazilites (meaning those who withdrew) who insisted that God alone is absolute unity. In their view, the Qur'an was certainly a primordial divine message but was a creature of God. To be uncreated means that it would rival God as absolute Being. The Mu'tazilites perceived a danger in equating the Qur'an with God, which in their mind would be analogous to Christianity in which Jesus is equated with God. As amazing as it may sound, the dogma of the uncreated nature of the Qur'an held sway and is maintained to this day.[40] The preparedness of Muslims to defend the sanctity of the Qur'an with their lives stems from this perception. The Qur'an is maintained as superior to any other revelation because in it we find the final speech of God, not because God has finished speaking, but because "he doesn't say anything new anymore."[41]

The divine nature the Qur'an means that the vessel, that is, the Prophet Muhammad, through whom or in which it was revealed has to be pure, in the same way in which the Virgin Mary is considered pure in Christian piety. Hence Muhammad is considered to have been illiterate *(ummi).*[42] He simply reported what he heard directly from the angel. The Qur'an, then, is not reported speech nor is it a message about a message, which is the way in which the Christian Scriptures are construed. Unlike some books of the Bible, it is not considered biographical. Rather, it is seen as "inimitable revelation, the speech of God revealed to the Prophet Muhammad . . . "[existing today] literally and orally in the exact wording of the purest Arabic."[43]

The revelation of the Qur'an in the Arabic tongue is another important issue to consider about the nature of the revelation. Surah 42:7 reads, "Thus have We sent by inspiration to thee an Arabic Qur'an." Yasuf 'Ali notes that the point of the revelation being in Arabic is that it is plain and intelligible to the people through whom and among whom it was promulgated.[44] There was no need for the people to whom the revelation came to translate the revelation. This is the logic of the Islamic practice for scholars to learn the language and so understand the revelation instead of attempting to translate the revelation into a different language, which carried with it the risk of losing its meaning. That which is said is inseparable from how it is said. As Cragg notes further, the language has a bearing on the import of the truth and the pattern of the truth is in the shape of the language.[45] "Every word is the word of God, and is comparable to what is found in the Bible along with the phrase 'thus says the Lord'."[46]

This perception of the Qur'an accounts for the view among Muslims that other languages cannot be the bearer of the fullness of the divine revelation. In modern discourse this point has often been missed because of the tendency to overlook the issue of revelation. However, as Comenius argued, God's wisdom and goodness demanded that his blessings should be widespread and not contained in a single language. For this reason, he included effective communication as one of the criteria for determining revealed scripture. In fact, one aspect of the reform of human affairs, with which he was concerned, was for the development of a common international language that would operate alongside the local national languages. This would facilitate communication between the nations and to provide a common means whereby the revelation of God could be read. The force and relevance of his position today is that unless the revelation of God was in a language that people could own and understand it would not be able to meet the intimate criterion of providing enlightenment or to pass judgement on the Christians and enlighten their darkness. He argued that Islam needed to rethink the notion that revelation from God can be apprehended only in a single language, which is one of the bases for insisting on the superiority of the Qur'an.

The revelation to the prophet seemed to have been in the oral tradition for only a short interval when compared with a somewhat long oral tradition in Christian scriptures. It was canonized within twenty-five years after the death

of Muhammad. One of the few analogies that can be accurately drawn between Christian and Muslim scriptures is between the compilation of the
Qur'an and that of an individual prophetic book in the Old Testament. The
prophetic messenger receives the word and must tell it as he received it. If he
does otherwise, he himself is under the indictment of the message he brings.
It cannot therefore be overstressed how differently scripture functions in the
two communities of faith.[47] For the Christian, the Bible, in which the revelation is recorded, derives its significance from Jesus Christ the revealed one.
However, for Islam, Muhammad, the bearer of the revelation, derives his significance from the revelation he brought.[48] Therefore, the significance of Jesus, for Christians, is similar to the significance of the Qur'an for Muslims.
We should therefore not seek to compare Jesus with Muhammad, even though
they are the leading personalities of the respective faith communities. The
comparison, rather, should be Jesus, on the one hand and the Qur'an on the
other. Muhammad is to be compared with the prophets, of whom he is believed to be the final. So even though the two faiths are concerned with revelation, they differ about the character and the content of the revelation, and
the way in which the revelation is communicated.[49]

Surah 96, which speaks about the revelation of the Qur'an, is believed to
be at least an early (if not the first) revelation given to Muhammad. This has
led to the observation in Muslim belief that the call of the Prophet Muhammad is coincident with the commencement of God's final speech to humanity. This in part explains why the recital of the Qur'an is so central to Islamic
life. The prophet recited the Qur'an, thus setting an example for the faithful.
When the faithful in Islam recite the Qur'an, they function in a manner analogous to the Prophet in declaring the mind of God to the world. This association of the Prophet with the Qur'an means that Muhammad and the Qur'an
play a critical role in Muslim piety. A full understanding of the Islamic faith
will, therefore, involve an appreciation of the role of the Prophet Muhammad,
which will be the focus of the next chapter.

NOTES

1. W. M. Watt, *Islamic Creeds: A Selection* (Edinburgh: Edinburgh University
Press, 1994), 4.
2. Knitter, *No Other Name*, 196.
3. *Nine Public Lectures*.
4. F. Esack, *Qur'an Liberation & Pluralism: An Islamic Perspective on Interreligious Solidarity Against Oppression* (Oxford: Oneworld, 19970), 257.
5. C. Le Gai Eaton, *Islam and the Destiny of Man* (London: George Allen & Unwin, 1985),3.

6. Eaton, *Islam*, 12.

7. See for example W. M. Watt, Islamic *Philosophy and Theology: An Extended Survey* (Edinburg: Edinburg University Press, 1985), 57. Watt shows that by 900 C.E. the four Sunnite Schools or rites, which still exist today, had fairly definite shape.

8. D. Shenk, *Global Gods: Exploring the Role of Religion in Modern Society* (Scottsdale, PA: Herald Press, 1995) p. 288.

9. A. H. Mahmud, *The Creed of Islam* (London: World of Islam Festival Trust, 1978), 13.

10. A. Schimmel, *Deciphering the Signs of God: A Phenomenological Approach to Islam* (Albany: New York State University Press, 1994), 246.

11. A. Rippin, *Muslims: Their Religious Beliefs and Practices Volume 1: The Formative Period* (London, New York: Routledge, 1990), 56.

12. K. Cragg, *The Call of the Minaret* (London: Collins, 1986), 31.

13. See also Surah 2:255; 59:22–23.

14. N. Daniel, *Islam and the West: The Making of an Image* (Oxford: Oneworld, 1993), 342ff.

15. O. Mohammed, S. J., *Muslim-Christian Relation: Past, Present, Future* (New York: Orbis Books, 1999), 60.

16. W. M. Watt, *Islam and Christianity Today: A Contribution to Dialogue* (London, Boston: Routledge & Kegan Paul, 1983), 2. The author insists on the differences of the understanding of God. The meaning of God in English or Allah in Arabic is determined not by its original meaning but by personal experiences and experiences within each faith community. Similarly, the Muslim-Christian Research Group holds that "Christian monotheism and Islamic monotheism are inherently different." See their publication, *The Challenge of the Scriptures: the Bible and the Qur'an* (Maryknoll, New York: Orbis Books, 1989), 74.

17. J. Henninger "Pre-Islamic Bedouin Religion" in M. Swartz, Ed., *Studies in Islam* (New York, Oxford: Oxford University Press, 1981), 12. The gods venerated at Mecca, al-Lat, al-Uzza and Manat, were termed daughters of Allah, but Allah played only a minor role in the actual cult. See also Cragg, *Call of the Minaret*, p. 31. Quoting Ryckmans, "Heaven and Earth in the South Arabian Inscriptions" *Journal of Semitic Studies* 3 (1958) pp. 225–36, Rippin notes that from the fourth and fifth centuries South Arabian inscriptions begun making mention of the monotheistic cult of Rahmanan, the Merciful, also qualified as Lord of heaven and earth. See Rippin, *Muslims: Their Beliefs and Practices*, 6.

18. See the dialogue between Josef van Ess and Kung in H. Kung, *Christianity and the World Religions: Paths of Dialogue with Islam, Hinduism and Buddhism* (London: Collins, 1987), 8.

19. H. Goddard, *Christians & Muslims: From Double Standards to Mutual Understanding* (Richmond, Great Britain: Curzon Press, 1995), 24. M. Rodison, "A Critical Survey of Modern Studies on Muhammad" in M. Swartz, Ed., *Studies in Islam*, p. 23, has shown where recent excavations and investigations by J. M. Sola Sole have revealed that monotheistic inscriptions have been found in Arabia dating as early as 493 C.E.

20. Kung, *Christianity and the World Religions*, 24.

21. Cragg, *The Event*, 65.

22. Cragg, *The Event*, 128. At a later stage we must look at the role of the Prophet Muhammad in determining the contours of the Islamic faith because it is difficult to consider the idea of God in Islam without reference to the prophet Muhammad.

23. Mahmud, *The Creed of Islam,* 37.

24. Cragg, *Call of the Minaret*, 31.

25. G. Parrinder, *Jesus in the Qur'an* (Oxford: Oneworld Publications, 1995), 26.

26. Watt lists factors relating to the association of the church with the Byzantine Empire, the use of Greek philosophy and total rejection of the so-called "heretics" as weaknesses that may have facilitated the spread of Islam in Christian regions. See his work *Muslim-Christian Relations*, p. 7.

27. Surah 4:171.

28. Parrinder, *Jesus in the Qur'an*, 134.

29. Watt, *Islam and Christianity Today*, 50.

30. Zinzendorf, *Twenty-One Discourses,* II, 21.

31. Kung, 121.

32. Kung, p. 111 makes reference to the work of Mahmoud M. Ayoub who puts the accent of the Qur'an's denial of the death of Jesus on the denial of the power of men to control and destroy the word of God. In *Muslim-Christian Relations*, p. 22; Watt holds the position that nearly all Muslims, from the time of Muhammad to the present, take Surah 4:156–8 and 3:55 to mean that Jesus did not die.

33. Parrinder, 116.

34. Dupuis, 253. The weakness with Dupuis' position, though, is that he fails to make the assertion concrete. Comenius, on the other hand, considers a specific tradition on the basis of criteria he proposes and to which he invites the particular tradition to subscribe.

35. Cragg, *The Event*, 26.

36. Schimmel, *Deciphering the Signs of God,* 161.

37. Schimmel, *Deciphering the Signs of God,* 151.

38. Kung, 15.

39. W. M. Watt, *Islamic Philosophy and Theology,* 58.

40. Schimmel, 155.

41. Josef van Ess in Kung, 15.

42. There seems to be growing consensus that *ummi*, which should be interpreted unlettered, refers to the fact that the immediate community for which Muhammad received the revelation was not in possession of a "book" in the sense in which the People of the Book (Jews and Christian) has their "book."

43. F. Esack, *Qur'an Liberation & Pluralism,* 53.

44. *The Meaning of the Holy Qur'an,* (Washington D.C.: Amana Publications, 1993), 1247, note 4533.

45. Cragg, *The Event*, 47.

46. Watt, *Islam and Christianity Today*, 57.

47. Goddard, *Christian & Muslim*, 40.

48. Daniel, 53.

49. Daniel, 11.

Chapter Four

The Qur'an and Muhammad in Islamic Piety

THE EXEMPLARY ROLE OF THE PROPHET

In the preceding chapter we considered beliefs that can be called essential beliefs in Islam and how these were related to Christian beliefs. We saw that beliefs by themselves are not the major driving force in Islam (or Christianity for that matter). Rather, ethical practice (praxis) are much more important than a doctrinal system. It is also true that most religious communities are known more by their ethical stances and the things they do and how they worship more than by their beliefs system. When the faithful put their beliefs and convictions into practice we call that piety. Muslim perceptions of the Qur'an and of the Prophet Muhammad influence Islamic piety at a very deep level. Muhammad is perceived as the messenger *par excellence* because he was the one who reported the Qur'an to Islam. The Qur'an, as we saw earlier, is God's final speech. In this chapter we shall give more attention to the role of the Prophet, as the first to demonstrate how the faith was to be practised and how he and the Qur'an function in the religious imaginations of the Islam.

It is hardly necessary to justify a focus on the role of the Prophet Muhammad in consideration of things essential in Islamic belief and piety. The exemplary role of the Prophet, which is rooted in the very essence of Islam, can be illustrated by the fact that Muslims follow his example not only to be wise but also to be obedient to the Qur'an. Cragg notes that obedience to the Prophet is steadily associated in the Qur'an with obedience to God and recognition of him as Prophet with recognition of God.[1] According to Cragg, he is the "norm of true behaviour and the unconscious source of the manners and total conduct of the community."[2] His significance is entrenched in the *Shahadah,* an article of faith that every mature believer in Islam is expected to

39

know. Yet, apart from the fact that he received the message of the Qur'an, "the absolute and undisputed point of reference . . . for Sunni Muslims [is] the Prophet's conduct."[3] His example "has illuminated the way and provided direction to his followers throughout the centuries,"[4] and he is the one who defined the borders of Islam as a separate religion.

Although the doctrine of salvation is more akin to Christian discourse than to Islam, we find that "Muhammad appears more and more as the intercessor who will intercede for the grave sinners."[5] From the point of view of the Islamic faith, he is the Muslim exemplar. This is borne out by the way he is portrayed in the Islamic creeds, which though they do not have the same status as the ecumenical creeds in Christianity, indicate what significant personalities at different era considered to be essential for the faith. These creeds have become classics in Islamic piety since Muslims today, with the probable exception of the Sufis, do not speak in a manner that suggests deification of the prophet. Nevertheless, the role of the prophet, as Muslim exemplar, is presented with the same force today as it was several generations ago. One example is the creed of Allama-I-Hilli, who was sage of Hilla (d. 1325). He refers to Muhammad as one who was immune from sin in a way that Christians refer to Jesus:

> He was immune from sin from the beginning of his life to the end of it, because people's heart would not be bound to obey one in whose past life various great and small sins and [other] hateful things had been observed.[6]

Another example is the creed of Al—Sanusi (d. 1486 or 1490). In article # 37 he says. "when we say Muhammad is the messenger of God that includes belief in all the other prophets and in the angels and in the heavenly book and the last day, since Muhammad came confirming the truth of all that."[7] Similarly, the creed of Al-Ghazali saw the role of Muhammad as coming from the wording of the *Shahadah*. According to Ghazali, "God . . . set Muhammad above the other prophets, and made him prince of the human race."[8]

In addition to the portrayal of the Prophet in the creeds of Islam, he is credited with the successful expansion of the faith in the first era of its existence. The writer J. Fueck observes that one is able to explain the unprecedented success of Islam "only if one takes into account the uniqueness of Muhammad's personality."[9] The turning point for the religion was the 622 C.E. migration of the Prophet from Mecca. As noted earlier, this movement out of Mecca had religious significance, but its political implications were of even greater value for the future of the faith. After the consolidation of a political and religious base at Medina, he returned to conquer Mecca, thus bringing it under Muslim rule. The subsequent successes in the expansion of Islam soon came to reinforce the self-understanding of Islam as God's final and decisive will for humankind.

After the successful capture of Syria in 634, the caliphates, inspired by Muhammad's example, went on to establish an empire, which rose like a phoenix from under the Sussanian and Byzantine empires. Rodison believes that successes in the eighth century were due primarily to the idea that Muhammad is God's Prophet. This belief that someone was pursuing the will of God in the conquest of other peoples, would later be used in the expansionist ideology of the European settlers in the Americas. The same idea also appeared to inspire the doctrine of Manifest Destiny that directed the policy of the American Empire in the nineteenth and twentieth centuries. According to Rodison, "this ideology prevented them [the Muslims] from being assimilated by the surrounding civilization."[10] Their military successes would later provide grounds for Christian polemic, in which Islam was seen as a religion that was spreading through conquest and the sword. With Islamic political organisations today willing to use the methodology of suicide bombings as a legitimate method of warfare, that medieval perception of Islam as a religion that promotes violence continues to influence popular perception of Islam. Persons speaking for Israel and America justify their vicious assaults on Islamic militants out of the fear that Islam is bent on conquering the world to subject it to the Islamic faith.

Muhammad should also be credited with helping to define the Islamic perception of Judaism and Christianity. In the thinking of early Muslims, Islam superseded Christianity, which had superseded Judaism. The successful expansion of Islam under Muhammad and the four caliphs that succeeded him would have reinforced this perception. The idea itself is derived from the Qur'an and consequently was the understanding of Muhammad himself. The references to the religions of the Book in the Qur'an, though, are enough evidence to suggest that both Judaism and Christianity have influenced Muhammad and Islam. The nature and extent of the influence has been the subject of several studies,[11] many of which were guided by partisan biases. While these biases may be seen as a counter-balance to the excesses to which the faithful in Islam tended to portray Muhammad, the observation by Cragg is probably the most apt description of the role of Muhammad. According to Cragg, Islam "grew out of Judaism and Christianity because it could not grow with them or into them."[12] It was Muhammad who led Islam out of and away from its precursors. However, the doctrine that Islam has superseded the other religions that were before it is an argument used by fewer Muslims today. Those who use it, as those in Christianity, who regard other religions as being of lesser value, are probably in the minority. The fact that Islamic leadership set ground rules for co-existence of Islam with other religions, particularly when Spain was in its control, is something that scholars often refer to as an example of Islamic sensitivity to religious pluralism.

Another aspect of Muhammad life that has continuing impact on Islamic life and piety is the *Sunna*, which is a collection of his sayings. These sayings can be regarded as his commentary in the Qur'an, which is the most reliable source for his life, theology and philosophy.[13] The message of God that he preached was also what he himself believed. The words of the Qur'an are the words of Muhammad, conveying the message he understood as spoken by the Angel Gabriel. The stories and examples of his life show that he was the best witness and example for the message he brought. It is not surprising, then, that after his death Muhammad was elevated to the highest level, being second only to God in Muslim piety.

Despite the clear influence that Muhammad has had in world religious history, and despite the obviously important inspiration he is to the Muslim faith, he remains somewhat of a problem from a traditional Christian point of view. Not only is he controversial but he is also sometimes portrayed in a very negative light in Christian literature. We must honestly face the reasons, especially in some Christian circles, for the negative attitude towards this popular religious figure. Norman Daniel, the author of the book, *Islam and the Making of the West*,[14] relies extensively on John of Damascus in developing his view of early Christianity. Nevertheless, he believes that in regard to Islam, the attitude of this early Christian leader was based on ignorance. Daniel sees this early Christian writer as the source of credible information about early Christianity but he believes that John of Damascus may be the founder of traditional Christian polemic against Islam and Muhammad, much of which was based on insufficient knowledge. The great problem with Islam, in medieval Christian eyes, was the claim of this younger religion to have superseded Christianity. This claim was bolstered by the fact that it did not take many years for Islam to replace Christianity as the leading religion in several European and Middle Eastern countries. Islam, therefore, was a victim of its own rapid growth as tensions and rivalries between the two religions were on a steady rise. For many Christians, Islam and the Prophet were seen as enemies of the Christ and Christendom. Like Daniel, Watt believes that the continuing influence of medieval caricatures on the perception of Islam today makes it difficult for Christians to freely embrace the prophethood of Muhammad.[15] The individuals associating themselves with Islam, who use unorthodox methods of warfare (like suicide bombing) to inflict revenge have exacerbated this negative perception. So with today's increase in the acts of terror, which people in the West are made to believe are carried out on the name of Islam, it is not hard to detect in modern times the same basic pattern of a relationship based on animosity, suspicion and fear.

However, the significant role of the Prophet Muhammad is not one of the negotiable items in Islam, which is not unique in the unwillingness to negotiate aspects of the Muslim faith. Judaism and Christianity also have some specific beliefs that they consider non-negotiable, or as Daniel terms it, "irreducible differences between non-negotiable doctrines."[16] For Judaism it is its unique chosen status, for Christianity it is the teaching of Christ as Son of God, for Islam, it is the Qur'an as the word of God and Muhammad as Allah's final prophet.[17] It should be noted that, as in the piety of Roman Catholicism and the Orthodox Churches, the Virgin Mary has a special place in Islam. The Virgin is respected in her role as the human conduit for the revelation of Jesus. In a similar way Muslims show honour and respect to the Prophet Muhammad because he is the human conduit for the revelation of the Qur'an. Muhammad was only a messenger *(rasul)*, through whom the message of the Qur'an was filtered. This means that the message was processed through the knowledge and conviction that he himself possessed. He did not relay a message against his conviction. It is hard, therefore, to make a distinction between the role of the prophet and the role of the Qur'an because it came through Muhammad, thus ensuring the eternal significance of the Prophet. Therefore, if Christians accept the Qur'an as a revealed word from God, they are obliged to accept Muhammad as a Prophet of God, since he is the messenger that brought that word. In other words, his prophetic calling must be judged on the basis of the message he brought and the fruits that accompany those who accept that message as one from God. However, this is a sticking point in the relationship between the two religions. There is not the readiness among most Christians to construe the Prophet Muhammad on the same level as the OT prophets, or even the apostles, much less Jesus.

Happily, not all sections of the Christian community make a negative assessment of Muhammad. For example, Kung stops short of declaring Muhammad a prophet by urging that Christians can take a number of positions concerning his role in the world, without conceding any point of doctrine concerning Jesus and Christianity. The first is that we can agree with the view that the people of the seventh century were justified in listening to Muhammad's voice. Secondly, we can say that Muhammad lifted them from polytheism to the heights of monotheism. Thirdly, we can affirm that people received from Muhammad (and the Qur'an) a boundless supply of inspiration to make a new departure in religion.[18] Kung believes these affirmations can help to resolve the problem of Muhammad in Christian eyes.

It seems, though, that the supreme difficulty with Muhammad's prophethood for Christians is that the community issuing from his preaching and practice purports to offer a message from God that abrogated all that went before it, thus making void the Christian message of Christ as God incarnate.

This is not a caricature, but represents the conflict in the very self-under-standings of the religions. Given the Christians' claim to revelation, a subse-quent claim of a similar nature must be seen as spurious. Since there is as yet no readiness on the part of the faithful Christian to negotiate on the person of Christ, then the resolution of the conflicts between the two religions must have a bearing on what Islam says about Jesus.[19] At the end of the day the Christian will naturally ask the non-Christian, "What do you say of the Christ?"

The discussion on the role of Muhammad cannot be neatly separated from the role of the Qur'an in Islamic piety, which we shall consider next. In con-sidering this issue, we shall also look at assertions made in or about the Qur'an that conflict with assertions in the Bible about similar events or per-sonalities. For example, it would be from Christian witnesses that the Islamic community learned of the birth, the death and the ministry of Jesus. The high place given to Mary in the Qur'an seems to be based on the role she is wit-nessed as playing in the New Testament. Moreover, Muhammad's prophetic calling is modelled after the OT prophets that preceded him. However, the ac-count in the Qur'an on these issues differ from the Biblical account. Muslim and Christian communities live with these differences, which have a bearing on how they relate and live with other differences in practice and self-under-standing. In a certain sense, then, sacred texts and how they are interpreted are central to Christian-Muslim relationship.

THE QUR'AN AND ISLAMIC PIETY

The belief in Islam that the Qur'an contains the most important revelation from God means that Muslims must of necessity elevate the Qur'an above all other sacred texts, including the Bible. It is because of the high esteem in which quranic revelations are held why the desecration or disrespect of the Qur'an is seen as an attack on the faith of Islam. The Qur'an symbolises the purity and perfection of the Islamic faith. For this reason, no secular docu-ment, for example the constitution of the country, can be given a pre-eminent place, if it contradicts or is in conflict with the Qur'an. There is an issue se-rious, then, in Islam, about whose interpretation of the Qur'an is to be ac-cepted as authoritative. When different group within Islam condemn each other, it often has to do with disagreement over how the Qur'an is interpreted. It is here on the point of interpretation (hermeneutics) that the discussion be-tween Islamic and Christian scholars is particularly lively.

One of the difficulties that some Christians have with the Qur'an is that some of its claims do not seem justifiable by any serious historical survey.

So, when we compare the Qur'an with the Bible, it is important to note that there are important differences of details in reference to similar events. The way in which the Muslims have dealt with the differences is to regard the earlier Christian scriptures as being corrupted at the points at which differences with the Qur'an occur. One such difference is the way in which Jesus is portrayed. In Parrinder's important work, *Jesus in the Qur'an,* for example, we can trace the names and the titles of Jesus. Parrinder finds that in referring to Jesus as spirit (*ruh*), the Qur'an employs a title that is not found of Jesus in the bible [Surah 4:171].[20] This, however, should not surprise us for the a certain mystery surrounds the account of the Jesus' death in the Qur'an. A forced interpretation of texts that associate Jesus with the Holy Spirit (for example John 20:22), may also claim that only one who is spirit can breathe the Holy Spirit. In this line of argument, one could also refer to the clause in the Western version of the Nicene Creed, which says that the Spirit "proceeds from the Father and the Son." Some Christian scholars, though would see any reference to Jesus as spirit as threatening to minimise his human life, death and resurrection, which are all fundamental aspects of the Christian faith.

Another area of conflict between the Qur'an and the Bible relates to the death of Jesus. Parrinder believes that on this question there are contradictory texts in the Qur'an itself. Surah 19:33, (Cf. Surah 19:15) reads, "So Peace is on me the day I was born, the day that I die, and the Day that I shall be raised up to life again." This text (Surah 19:33) is said to contradict Surah 4:157, which specifically says, "they killed him not." Some Muslim commentators see 19:33 as a reference to the future death of Jesus. Parrinder notes, however, that the grammar of the text does not indicate a future sense.[21] Yasuf 'Ali in his commentary on Surah 4:157 notes that like Muslims, "some early Christian sects did not believe that Christ was killed on the cross."[22] Yasuf 'Ali, although maintaining that Jesus was not crucified,[23] calls the end of Jesus' life on earth a mystery.

CONFLICTS BETWEEN THE BIBLE AND THE QUR'AN

Some Muslims today still refer to the doctrine of corruption (*tahrif*) when accounting for differences between the Bible and the Qur'an. The fundamental nature of this issue for Christians makes important to develop a Christian response. For Muslims the matter is quite simple: the Qur'an is the infallible scripture and all that is true agrees with it. Since the Bible does not agree with it, they then hold that the Bible must be corrupt. The logic of this argument, according to Cragg, is predicated on "a hypothesis that is beyond proof or disproof."[24] The precise formulation of this doctrine, according to Watt, is somewhat elusive; sometimes meaning that the actual text of the Bible was altered, and at other times meaning that the interpretation was changed.[25] However, considering that the Christian Canon was fixed three centuries before the dawn of Islam, it is difficult to put in the mind of the authors of those scriptures an anti-Islamic intent, when they would not have known of Islam. From a Christian point of view, then, the Qur'an needs to be subjected to the kind of critique to which the Bible has been subjected. It is only in this way the glaring discrepancies between the accounts, especially concerning Jesus, can be overcome. In comparing the picture of Jesus in the Qur'an with that in the Bible Kung describes the portrayal of Jesus in the Qur'an as "ill-defined and void of substance."[26] He sees a danger in seeking to maintain the verbal inspiration dogma. Maintaining that dogma means, "the Qur'an faces a long term danger from the breakdown of what sociologists call its plausibility structure."[27] A revision of that dogma, to the extent that that is possible, may serve to lead the Qur'an out from under the suspicious cloud that hangs over it. We can hardly avoid the conclusion that from a historical point of view, the text of the Qur'an is suspect at the point where it denies the death of Jesus. Muslims must then be challenged to revisit their claims about Jesus that deny what is mentioned in the Bible and otherwise corroborated by secular history.

The problematic nature of the discrepancies in the Qur'an arises from the way in which the revelation it brings is construed. When the words, which are human words, are the content of the revelation, they have a very vulnerable existence, being subjected to the vicissitudes of human use, misuse and interpretation. Any attempt, then, to render the letter of the text as absolute "is a surrendering of the ineffable character of the transcendent word of God."[28] Farid Esack has highlighted in his book *Qur'an Liberation and Pluralism* the problems and burdens associated with interpreting a text whose author is none other than God himself. According to Esack, "it is inconceivable that Muslims would claim to get into the mind of God."[29] Yet, this is precisely what the idea of authorship by God requires of one who would make sense of the revelation. The one who reads it must get a sense of the mind of God. The Qur'an is the undisputed reference point for Muslims, but the unavoidable point of departure for approaching this criterion is "one's self and the condition wherein that self is located."[30] The word of God must then become a word filtered through the gauze of human experience. We cannot then avoid reference to the socio-political context when reading the message that the Prophet Muhammad brought.

The question of the language of the Qur'an, which is another issue of Islamic piety, was mentioned earlier. Muslims believe that the purest form of the revelation subsists in the Arabic language, which amounts to suggesting that the language of God is Arabic and that the thought of God is in Arabic alone. Such a line of reasoning is not far from saying that God is an Arab, a thought that is reprehensible to Muslims and non-Muslims alike. The calcification of the revelation in Arabic implies a significant limitation on God's part. This should not be interpreted to mean that the problem of interpretation is any less critical for the Christian, who, according to 1Cor 2:16, may claim to "have the mind of Christ." The difference in the Christian account of revelation, however, is that God's self-disclosure is in a person, Jesus the Christ, with whom a relationship can be built. The self-disclosure is symbolic of God's movement towards humanity, and the intention of God to be known in the reality of human experience without censorship. The Christian scripture is the account of not one but of several witnesses who span several centuries: "the eighteen or so centuries between Abraham and St. John."[31] They testify to that ongoing self-disclosure of God. An interpretative task and a process of incarnation are, therefore, presumed to be always happening in authentic experiences of God. It could be argued that the insistence on the purity of the revelation in the Arabic language means the language of the Qur'an functions as a means by which God's revelation is censored. Maybe a more realistic position than that the Qur'an abrogated the message of the Bible is that it needs the Bible to corroborate its message.

Perhaps the most important issue that Christians must consider is that "the Qur'an, despite the constraint of the purity of the revelation in Arabic, has sustained and continues to sustain today, an immense cry of faith in the one God."[32] Christians can then treat the Qur'an as an extra-canonical material that is of theological value; a message brought by a man of God, the Prophet Muhammad. That message could not make it into the Christian canon because, apart from the discrepancies concerning Jesus, it came after the Christian canon was closed.

The contributions of Christians in recent scholarship in interfaith studies have tended to argue for changes in Christian exclusiveness as a way of healing the rift between religions.[33] This trend of moving towards changes in Christian self-understanding has resulted in changes in perception of the Jews. This is seen, for example in the way the Roman Catholic Church now speak of the Jews in their official statements. The Church no longer speaks of Christianity as superseding Judaism, as used to be the case before Vatican II. The authenticity of the Jewish faith is fully respected.[34] It is possible for a similar development to occur in the relationship with Islam. Christians, who wish to use the language of "uniqueness," should understand that they can think of themselves as being unique to God but they cannot insist that God is unique to them. For God to be God he must be free to reveal himself to those he wishes in the manner he wills. One approach could be for the idea of exclusiveness to be attached to the individual's relationship with God rather than to God.

The assertion of exclusiveness has tended to exacerbate tensions between Muslims and Christians and there seems is a direct relationship between Muslim exclusiveness and anti-Muhammad polemic. However, many Muslims, being anxious to lessen the tension, have already dropped the idea that Islam superseded Christianity. They recognise that changes in Muslim self-understanding will have an impact on how the religion and the Prophet are perceived. Christians should also consider whether the anti-Christian posture in many Islamic communities is not, likewise, related the unnecessary Christian exclusivism that some Christians continue to hold.

Let us then summarize the argument above: Muslims regard the Qur'an as being entirely from God with neither the personality of Muhammad nor the early leaders having anything to do with. However, when comparisons are made between the Bible and the Qur'an several inconsistencies are spotted on several important details. One response by Muslims is to say that the Bible was corrupted in its transmission. Given the existence of these discrepancies and the fact that the Bible account is in some places corroborated by secular history, the question arises whether the belief of biblical corruption is defensible. What then is to be the attitude of the Christian to the idea that the Qur'an is God's final speech? Cragg suggested that we consider "the Qur'an as "definitive, but not exclusive, final but not total."[35] This is a hopeful suggestion because the perception of the Qur'an as definitive but not exclusive already exists in the practice of Islamic law *(Shari'a)*. The legal luminaries of Islam will use another authoritative body of material, called the *Hadith, as well as* the Qur'an, in legal proceedings. From a legal point of view, therefore, the Qur'an is neither final nor definitive.

The imperfect perception of Christianity in the Qur'an should not blind the Christian to the otherwise positive values of its teachings. However, if the Muslim-Christian Research Group is right in their observation, then we see that a mere positive appraisal of its teachings is insufficient. The Group's position is that "in the Qur'an everything is oriented to the proclamation of the oneness of God."[36] Conversation between Christians and Muslims should not miss this point, which is something around which a common position can emerge. What is clear is that despite their difficulties, the oneness of God, the Qur'an as God's final speech and the exemplary role of the Prophet Muhammad, are essential to Muslim self-understanding.

Having considered the essentials in Islam, our corresponding task is to look at the essentials in Christian self-understanding.

NOTES

1. *The Event*, 37.
2. Cragg, *The Event*, 93.
3. Esack, 75.
4. Fueck, "The Originality of the Arabian Prophet" *Studies in Islam*, 97.
5. Schimmel, p. 190. See also Rippin, *Muslims: Their Beliefs and Practice,* 43.
6. Watt, *Creeds*, 99ff.
7. Watt, *Creeds*, 90.
8. Watt, Creeds, 73ff; article #15.
9. J. Fueck, "The Role of Traditionalism in Islam" in M. Swartz, Ed., *Studies in Islam,* p. 100.
10. M. Rodison, "A Critical Survey of Modern Studies on Muhammad," *Studies in Islam,* 52.
11. In addition to the article by Rodison, see also Fueck, "The Originality of the Prophet," *Studies in Islam*, 86–98.
12. *The Event*, 63.
13. Rodison, "A Critical Survey," 39.
14. Norman, *Islam and the West: The Making of An Image* (Oxford: One World, 1993), 13.
15. Watt, Islam and Christianity Today, 60–61.
16. Daniel, 335–6.
17. Kung, 36.
18. Kung, 27.
19. R. Haight, *Jesus Symbol of God* (Maryknoll, New York: Orbis Books, 1999), is an example of this.
20. Parrinder, 50. Parrinder also refers to Surah 2:87; 2:253; 5:110 as instances where Jesus is referred to as Spirit. However, the translation and commentary by A Yasuf 'Ali does not lead to that understanding. See *The Holy Qur'an*, 40, note 90 and 104, note 289.
21. Parrinder, 105.
22. *The Holy Qur'an,* 236, note 663.
23. Some commentators have noted that Muslims hold that the Jews did not kill Jesus, which is the clear implication of the Qur'an in Surah 4: 157. However, it is not just that the death of Jesus at the hands of the Jews is denied. Muslims deny that Jesus died any at all.
24. Cragg, *Call of the Minaret*, 254.
25. Watt, *Islam and Christianity*, 2.
26. Kung, 111.
27. Kung, 33.
28. *The Challenge of the Scriptures*, 16.
29. Easck, 73–75.
30. Esack, p. 75.
31. Cragg, *Call of the Minaret,* 251.

32. *The Challenge of the Scriptures*, 67.

33. See P. Knitter, *No Other Name?: A Critical Survey of Christian Attitudes Towards the World Religions* (London: SCM, Maryknoll: Orbis Books, 1985), J. Hick and B. Hebblethwaite, Eds., *The Myth of Christian Uniqueness: Towards a Pluralistic Theology of Religions* (Maryknoll, New York: Orbis Books, 1987).

34. This was given impetus by the Vatican II Declaration on other Religions.

35. Cragg seems to understand "finality" not in a linear but functional sense. "[The finality of the Qur'an] is its creative relevance, [and] its vital applicability." See *The Event*, 123 and 179.

36. Muslim-Christian Research Group, *The Challenge of the Scriptures*, 71.

Chapter Five

Christian Essentials and Muslim Questions

THE NATURE OF THE PROBLEM

Determining what may be called essential doctrines is no less difficult for Christianity than it is for Islam. This difficulty is not ameliorated by the existence of creeds and affirmations of faith that summarize beliefs, because they are usually developed in polemic relationship with others who may not share their ideals. Moreover, there are many Churches that do not regard themselves as credal. This means that they do not subscribe to any particular creed, as being definitive of the faith they profess. As is the case in Islam, many Christian groups do not accept any other authority for the interpretation of the sacred texts other than themselves. The tendency to rely on one's own authority for the understanding of the Bible and the Qur'an in part accounts for the development of extremism within the faith communities. In this chapter we shall look at doctrines that Christians consider as being essential to their faith and what it means to affirm them among Muslims. In order to avoid gross generalisation, however, an attempt will be made to locate the confession of these doctrines within a concrete religious community. This reinforces the point that was made earlier that when a Muslim meets a Christian the latter is usually from a specific religious denominational tradition, with a unique history. The Muslim who seeks to develop an understanding of Christianity must route the development of their perception through a particular religious tradition. In other words, the Muslim will need to understand that Christianity is particularised in specific religious communities, some of which have extensive disagreements between them.

Developing a confession of faith represents an attempt by a religious community to define itself, and may be a good starting point in coming to an understanding of that community. In developing a confession of faith, the religious community delineates those principles and beliefs by which they wish to be known and by which they intend to live. However, that which is set out in a confession often precedes the actual practice that a person from a different faith will first encounter. Even churches that refuse to be defined by particular creed have emphases within its life and practices by which it can be identified.

Consider for example the Moravian Church, which is a point of reference in this study. In its ancient manifestation it had a Confession of Faith that was revised thirty-four times between 1460 and 1658.[1] The revisions reflected the changes that took place in how the Church wanted to be understood in light of the changing context in which it existed. The Confession of 1535 was one of the more important for that religious community because they needed to establish the differences between them and the emerging Lutheran community, which they closely resembled. By seeking to define itself over against Lutheranism, the Moravian Church gave the appearance of vacillating in theology "between sheer Lutheranism and a sort of Brethrenism stimulated by Lutheran thought."[2] During the period 1727 to 1760 (which can be called Zinzendorfian period, after the most outstanding leader of the period) the church, particularly the German Province, turned to the Augsburg Confession, as its defining confession, believing it to be the most comprehensive statement of the Christian faith. Eventually, the Church abandoned creeds of its own, believing that they were not adequate descriptions of the mystery of salvation, which the church wanted to communicate, and as such should not be followed slavishly. While subscribing to a number of creeds,[3] therefore, the Church echoes the convictions of previous eras, affirming that, "the mystery of Jesus Christ which is attested to in the Bible, cannot be comprehended completely by any human statement."[4] Consequently, the Church's Book of Order (in the section on "The Ground of the Unity") makes no references to specific doctrines, as in earlier editions.

However, even with the refusal to select particular doctrines for emphasis, the Church found that it was still necessary to give some indication of its attitude to scripture, its attitude to the world and, most importantly, its belief about Jesus. By seeking to resolve these concerns, the church was being consistent with the doctrinal emphases in its early history, in which there was a demarcation of those doctrines considered as being necessary for salvation. The move illustrates that the core beliefs and practices of a Christian church can be broadly organised into three areas: belief about scripture, belief about Jesus and belief about the world in which we live. A careful analysis shows that to be the case for a wide cross-section of Christian communions. In the sections that follow we shall then focus on these three areas, in the context of a conversation with Islam. The issues we shall consider in turn are the primary authority of scripture, the centrality of Jesus and public witness or service in the world. We will show how these issues came into prominence in the Christian community and hence why an understanding of Christian belief can benefit from seeing the role they have played in shaping the life of a particular Christian communion.

THE PRIMACY OF SCRIPTURE

The affirmation of the divine character of the Bible has a long history in defining Christian self-understanding. The different positions that are presently adopted across Christian Churches may in fact have as their fountainhead the turmoil in the Roman Catholic Church in the fifteenth century. Drawing on the teachings of Wycliffe, John Hus, the founder of the Hussite Movement, emphasised the importance of scripture as final authority in matters of doctrine and practice. When controversy broke out between the Pope and the leadership of the Church in Czechoslovakia in the early fifteenth century, the Emperor intervened to facilitate a conversation, in a bid to ameliorate the impending religious split in the kingdom. In seeking to make their position clear, the Hussite developed what they called the *Four Articles of Prague*.[5] Their significance is that it was one of the earliest attempts to articulate the role that scripture would play in intra-church conflict in the coming years. In the first of the *Four Articles of Prague*, which were promulgated in 1521, the Hussite demanded free access to the Word of God. The significance of this attempt is that emphasis was considered important because of the practice that emerged in the Catholic Church where the individual study of scripture was not encouraged among the laity. This tiny religious stream of scriptural primacy in Bohemia would later become a mighty river by the time of the Lutheran Reformation, in which the doctrine of *sola scriptura* (scripture alone) became a central tenet.

One should not suppose that Roman Catholicism did not also have an emphasis on scripture. However, that emphasis on scripture was balanced by an emphasis of the tradition of the church, in which scripture was preserved and handed on to later generations. The idea in modern Protestantism of giving scripture a more pre-eminent place than the tradition of the church was lifted up by the Moravians and later expanded by Luther. For the Moravians, the Old and New Testaments bear witness to the revelation of the triune God. The Church Order of the Moravian Church states that:

> Scripture is the sole standard of the doctrine and faith of the Unitas Fratrum and therefore shapes [its] life. . . . But just as Holy Scripture has not developed any doctrinal system, so the Unitas Fratrum has not developed any of its own. . . . All creeds . . . stand in need of constant testing in light of the Holy Scriptures.[6]

This wording, "Scripture is the sole standard of the doctrine and faith of the Unitas Fratrum and therefore shapes [its] life," was formally accepted at the

Synod of 1857. This emphasis, however, is in fact based on an Augustinian emphasis that Hus picked up but was already found in the writings of Peter Lombard.[7] For the early Moravians, true faith is to believe God (*credere Deo*), because of the revelation through God's word. The scriptures are to be revered "as the Word of God, which he spake to mankind, in time past by the prophets."[8] Dead faith is to believe that God "has revealed himself through His Word, but not to believe in God."[9] Repeating the wording of the Moravian Synod of 1879, the Church declared in 1888 that in scripture, "all truths that declare the will of God for our Salvation are fully contained."[10] Karl Barth, who was probably the most influential theologian of the twentieth century, picked and expanded this notion of the Word of God, which "comes in the form of indicative and prescriptive utterances, which seek belief and obedience rather than unbelief or doubt."[11]

The authority of scripture relates also to its interpretation, which is critical to the determination of sound teaching and doctrine. For this reason most religious communities have particular conventions for ensuring reliable and accurate interpretation. In the early Moravian tradition, it was declared that there were secret things in scripture, and that "it [was] not our business to determine what Holy Scripture has left undetermined."[12] As the Synod of 1879 declared, the mysteries of scripture "are impenetrable to human reason."[13] Zinzendorf, Bishop of the Moravian Church (d.1760) held this understanding of scripture. According to him, some truths of scripture are clear and binding on all and there are other truths that are not so plain, in which differences of interpretation must be allowed.[14] However, in more recent editions of the Church Order the reference to mysteries has been replaced by a reference to the history of interpretation: "in interpreting Scripture . . . we look to two millennia of ecumenical Christian tradition and wisdom of our Moravian forbears . . . to guide us."[15] It is nevertheless maintained that the mystery of Jesus Christ is beyond complete comprehension by any human mind. This limitation put on human reason was necessary to come to terms with the challenge to Moravian self-understanding that was posed by the Enlightenment, which "subverted all claims to unchangeable authority and subjected all traditions, including those of Scripture, to critical scrutiny."[16]

The "Word of the Cross as the centre of Holy Scripture,"[17] which is a key to interpreting all scripture, has a long tradition in Moravian hermeneutics. The Church Manual declares that the testimony of Jesus' death "is the beginning, middle and end of our ministry,"[18] and proclaiming the Lord's death is the main calling of the Brethren's Church. The ecumenical movement would later come to this understanding of the centrality of the redemptive activity of Jesus as a necessary presupposition of biblical interpretation.[19] The hermeneutical key of the Lord's death is alluded to in others ways in which scripture is described. In the *1503 Apology,* scripture is declared as inspired (as in 2 Timothy 3:16) and bears witness to the essentials concerning the merits of Christ's grace. In an unusual reference, Maynard mentions that the 1573 Confession uses the term infallible to describe scriptures: "they are true, infallible and worthy of all belief, having been inspired by the Holy Ghost."[20] However, the Results of the Synod of 1632 and subsequent years do not use this terminology, which implies that the idea of infallibility, which is central to the teaching of some Christian churches, does not belong to the longer tradition of Moravian discourse on scripture. In fact, Schultze, a leading interpreter of Moravian doctrine in the twentieth century notes: "it must be admitted that here and there, in the Bible, the human element includes traces of human error in minor matters of historical detail."[21] However these errors do not compromise the fact that scripture is a trustworthy record of the great truths of divine revelation for the salvation of humanity.

One can see from above that there are many point of convergence between Christians and Muslims that have been recognised. Both faith communities understand God as Creator and Sustainer, and as the one who reveals his word and will to the human being. This convergence is derived from the scriptural revelation in their respective traditions. The role of the Bible in Christian piety is similar in some respects to the role that the Qur'an plays in Muslim piety. However, Whaling has argued that scripture has a wider importance for Islam than it does for Christianity.[22] He sees the Bible "as part of an evolution of scripture in book form . . . that culminated in Islam singling out the 'religions of the book'."[23] By its reference to the scriptural traditions of other religions, Islam was positioning itself as the guardian of that tradition,[24] because Muslims regard the Qur'an as the pinnacle of God's revelation. Christianity makes a similar claim, to the effect that the Bible bears witness to the final revelation of God in the person of Jesus Christ. The affirmation of finality of the revelation in Jesus Christ, which Christians make, is analogous to the Muslim claim of finality of the revelation in the Qur'an.

Thus in regarding scripture as normative for faith and theology and the most trustworthy deposit of things needful for salvation, Christians should be able to appreciate and understand the attitude Muslims have to their scriptures. Yet this attitude implies a rejection of Christ as the centre of God's revelation. Interfaith relations require that the statuses of these claims be revisited. A major problem of the relationship between Christianity and Islam is whether it is possible to have a Christian account of God's revelation and a way of reading scripture, which does not make null and void the revelation of the Qur'an. Furthermore, how will Christians regard Muslims' account of revelation in light of the centrality of Jesus Christ for their self-understanding? We turn now to consider the centrality of Jesus in Christian piety, which has a bearing on these questions.

THE CENTRALITY OF JESUS

The christocentrism of modern Protestantism is due largely to the influence of Count Zinzendorf (1700–1760), who engineered the revival of pietism in the early eighteenth century. The pietistic movement reaches back to the seventeenth century Johann Arndt's *True Christianity* and Phillip Jakob Spener's *Pia Desideria,* the works of Gottfried Arnold and Gerhard Tersteegen, all of which were concerned to raise the quality of Christian living to a higher level. These texts are regarded as setting the foundation of the thought of the movement.[25] Arndt embraced a theology that emphasised asceticism and mystical union with God but which was opposed to theological speculation. For him theology was not a mere science or rhetoric but a living experience and practice. True Christianity consists, "not in word or external show, but in [a] living faith, from which arise righteous fruits."[26]

The leading school of pietism in Europe during the time of Zinzendorf was the University of Halle in Germany, where Christian Wolf was lecturing on the virtue of Enlightenment rationalism for theology. By calling Christians to centre their thoughts on Jesus, Zinzendorf was responding to the Enlightenment's attack on revealed religion. The period of the Enlightenment was a time in which the traditional perception of the world was shaken by new scientific discoveries. Support for revelation declined as the space for the divine in the world begun to shrink. Indeed, it could be argued also that Zinzendorf's critique of rationalism was counter-balanced by the excessive claims to knowledge, which he saw in his Enlightenment context. Zinzendorf asserted that the love shed abroad in the heart by the Holy Spirit, which was concretized in the incarnation and the death of Jesus, was a truth that philosophy could not comprehend.[27]

In his own brand of christocentrism, Barth asserted that obedience to God in his essence means becoming obedient to Jesus.[28] It is also from Barth that we get the view that religions reflect the attempt of human beings to reach God whereas it is by faith that we see that in Jesus God has reached down to the world.[29] Barth throws his theological weight behind Zinzendorf's position by claiming him as "perhaps the only genuine Christocentric of the modern age."[30] For Barth, Zinzendorf is the true genius of the evangelical awakening of the nineteenth century.[31]

The pre-eminence of christology, which we see in Zinzendorf, was also evident in the earliest period of the Moravian Church. In fact, one could say that christology was the prism through which one had to look in order to under the Trinity. This is evident in the *Apology* of 1503, in which the belief concerning God was seen to depend on the revelation of Christ. According to the *Apology*, "The Brethren believe concerning God the Father that He begot His only Son . . . gave Him for the redemption of the world, and works salvation through his merits."[32] The Holy Ghost proceeds not solely from the Father as in the original wording of the Nicene Creed, but from both the Father and the Son.[33] Similarly, in response to the question, "What is God the Father?" the 1522 Catechism gives the answer, "God the Lord having a Son coequal in the Godhead."[34]

The hymns of Christian piety also reflect the centrality of Jesus in the imagination and practice of the faith. The verses below are from hymns written by Zinzendorf:

> O Spirit of grace, thy kindness we trace
> In showing to us, that life and salvation proceed from Christ's cross.
> In darkness we strayed until we were led
> By thee to believe that Jesus our saviour will sinners receive. . .
> O Therefore impart thyself to each heart
> That thus we may show, in our whole behaviour that Jesus we know.[35]

> The Saviour's blood and righteousness my beauty is, my glorious dress;
> Thus well arrayed, I need not fear, when in his presence I appear . . .
> Lord, I believe thy precious blood, which at the mercy-seat of God
> For ever doth for sinners plead, for me, even my soul was shed.
> Lord, I believe, were sinners more than sands upon the ocean shore,
> Thou has for all a ransom paid, for all a full atonement made.[36]

> In thee we live by faith, Jesus our God and Saviour;
> On thy atoning death our souls shall feed for ever:
> Thy suffering shall remain deep on our hearts impressed,
> Thou Son of God and man, till we with thee shall rest.[37]

For Count Zinzendorf, knowledge of Christ must always be seen in light of the cross.[38] This emphasis on the atoning work of Christ was related to his understanding of the human being, who was seen as being totally depraved on account of the fall and is thus unable to save himself. Salvation for the individual could only be found in the reconciling sacrifice of Jesus Christ. It was Zinzendorf's view that the historical presentation of God in Christ gives the Christian a better view of God than can be found in other religions.[39] So emphatic was the focus on Jesus that Zinzendorf was criticized for leaving aside the fundamental doctrine of the Trinity. In a polemic work published in 1753, Henry Rimius takes Zinzendorf to task over his doctrine of the Trinity. He claimed that:

> According to Zinzendorf . . . creation and sanctification ought not to be ascribed to the Father and the Holy Ghost. To avoid idolatry, people ought to be taken from the Father and [the] Holy Ghost, and conducted to Christ, with whom alone we have to do. The Ancients never dreamt of a Trinity.[40]

The radical christocentrism of Zinzendorf was also evident in the Catechism prepared for persons going on the mission field. In response to the question what is the name of the maker of mankind, the answer given was "Jesus

Christ."[41] The doctrine of salvation for Zinzendorf was simply that the creator Jesus Christ, who enfleshed himself as man, is Saviour.[42] He seemed to have understood references to God in the Hebrew Bible as references to Jesus.

Even though he made novel interpretations that did not conform to the earlier Moravian tradition, Zinzendorf never departed from belief in the Trinity. He preferred for example to say that "Christ reconciled God" instead of "Christ reconciled the Father," so as not to appear to be setting up a hierarchy within the Godhead.[43] In his emphasis on missions, Zinzendorf held that it was Jesus who revealed the Trinity, since it is Jesus who is the mediator between God and human beings.[44] In his understanding, the Holy Spirit functioned as a mother because of the Spirit's role in conversion and the shaping of Christian life and community.[45] He refused however to speculate on the character of the relationships within the Trinity because scripture was silent on the question.

The result of the christocentric focus was the absence of the traditional discourse of the Father, Son and Holy Ghost in Moravian theology. In the Synods of the nineteenth century, an attempt was made to reintroduce the Trinitarian nuances of an earlier period, as seen for example in the 1857 Compendium of Doctrine. There we find statements on the doctrine of the real Godhead and the real manhood of Jesus, who is the incarnation of God, the Creator of all things. The Holy Spirit is not spoken of proceeding from Jesus, but from the Father.[46] Nevertheless, the chief doctrine "over which [the Church] kept guard as a priceless jewel [was] that Jesus Christ is the propitiation for sins."[47] It was in this spirit that Blanford writing in 1930 said that the second "essential" is "in non-essentials, liberty" but that the first essential is "Jesus Christ, the Saviour of the World."[48]

QUESTIONS ABOUT JESUS

Christians should be aware, however, that increasingly the traditional Chalcedonian Christology and the doctrine of the incarnation are coming in for questioning, and not primarily from Muslims. This questioning, coming particularly from among Christians, is not an acceptance of the lower status of a mere prophet that is ascribed to Jesus in Islam, but reflects a difficulty with the traditional understanding of the incarnation. Such difficulties as those Christian theologians point to, give credence to Josef van Ess's view that the idea of the Trinity is a logical nonsense.[49] The re-thinking of the meaning of incarnation was significantly advanced by John Hick's work, *The Myth of God Incarnate*. Following Hick, others have argued that there is no justification for maintaining the uniqueness of Jesus' incarnation.[50] Stubenrauch has suggested that there are two reasons for this questioning of the traditional Christian belief in the incarnation. In the first place, the belief that God is able to touch humanity in any way is disputed. Thus, "God becomes a little more than a hostage to his own immensity."[51] Secondly, there is the view that humanity is basically incapable of embracing divinity. The ineffability of God renders humanity helpless, so the idea of an incarnation should not be understood to mean a total representation of all that God is.[52] If Christians were able to come to terms with this *de facto* Islamic theology within Christian theology, it would go a long way in relating the centrality of Christ to Islam's account of revelation.

It is not only the claims that Christians make about Jesus that give Muslims reasons for concern but also the practices of Christian missionaries. Tensions arise because both Christians and Muslims are missionary oriented religions. The character of Christian witness in the world, which is considered fundamental to the practice of the Christian faith, is therefore another area on which the relationship between Islam and Christianity should focus. The Moravian Church, for example, regards itself as existing Church for the purpose of serving Jesus Christ who calls the Church into being. The reason for the calling is service in the world. This idea of service to Jesus by serving in the world is therefore a critical aspect of Moravian self-understanding. We shall now consider the extent to which this missionary understanding of Christians impact on the relationship with Islam.

DIAKONIA–CHRISTIAN WITNESS AND SERVICE

The fact that Christians and Muslims together account for nearly half the population of the world means that the nature of the relationship between these two religious communities will impact significantly on the state of affairs in the world. It may be that the increasing sense of insecurity in several capitals of the world will be most significantly mitigated with greater attention paid to how Muslims and Christians bear witness internally in their own communities and to each other. Muslims will overcome the suspicion they have of the philanthropic work of Christians when they pursue a diakonical form of witness that has its own integrity.[53]

Churches generally make service to the world a part of their official book of Order. In the case of the Moravian, for example, the Book of Order is replete with references to service in the world, as the reason for which the Moravian Church exists. One such reference states that:

> The Unitas Fratrum is, therefore, aware of its being called in faith to serve humanity . . . Jesus Christ came not to be served but to serve. From this each

Church receives its mission and power for service, to which each member is called. We believe that the Lord has called us particularly to mission service among peoples of the world . . . Jesus Christ maintains in love and faithfulness His commitment to this fallen world. Therefore we must remain concerned for this world. We may not withdraw from it through indifference, pride or fear.[54]

It was this self-understanding of service that fired the ambition of the missionaries of the eighteenth and nineteenth centuries. The first two missionaries set out in 1732 "with six dollars . . . determined to sell themselves as slaves if there were no other way of preaching the gospel to the Negroes."[55] Hasse reports that after twenty-five years the Herrnhut village had sent more than one hundred missionaries to fields around the world.[56] When the Centennial Anniversary of the Moravian Society for Propagating the Gospel was held in 1887, Rev. J. Taylor Hamilton reported that after one hundred years twenty-two hundred (2200) persons had been commissioned to the mission field.[57] At that time three hundred and forty missionaries were serving in one hundred and twenty-three locations worldwide. The persistence in service continued despite aborted projects in Lapland, Algiers, Ceylon, Guinea, Persia, Egypt, East Indies and Demerara, among others. One project that symbolized the commitment of the whole Unitas Fratrum to service is the Leper Home that was established in Jerusalem in 1865. This work is particularly important, not only because the project has made an outstanding contribution towards the elimination of leprosy, but also because it has been primarily among Muslims. The Director of the Home reported in 1924 that, "for more than a century the Moravian Church has tried, in various ways, to help . . . first in Africa, then in Jerusalem and Surinam."[58] Of the eighty lepers that were believed to be in Palestine in 1926, thirty of them (26 of whom were Muslims) were under the care of the Moravians.[59] Consistent with this commitment to service, the first principle mentioned in the 1887 Centennial as under-girding these enterprises in mission was the following:

> The Moravian Church has ever made it its purpose to preach the Gospel to the most degraded, most neglected and most despised. . . . This has an immense bearing upon the problem of self-support, because it indicates how low down in the scale of humanity the Moravian Mission protégés have been. . . . The ultimate purpose has always been to establish an indigenous Church.[60]

This self-understanding of commitment to service is also the survival of a kind of puritanical work ethic from the Ancient Unity. In view of the fact that the early Moravians defined themselves over against the excesses of life associated with the Roman Church, they went to great pains to obliterate all signs of extravagance and debauchery. Certain occupations, for example dice manufacturing, theatrical profession and astrology were forbidden, as well as involvement in public amusement. Emphasis was put on caring for the poor and the sick, so that the Brethren would show themselves to be a peculiar people. The ministers were expected to be examples of holy living and industry. All members of the church, likewise, from the manor-lords to serfs and servants "were carefully regulated with a view to industry, to honesty and to the glory of God."[61] Thus Moravian commitment to service has been influenced by a pre-reformation puritanical work ethic practiced in Bohemia, and the Pietistic missionary zeal that swept across Germany in the early parts of the eighteenth century.

The character and content of Christian missionary activities must be revisited, if the sometimes-contentious relationships between Muslims and Christians are to be alleviated. Both religions see themselves as having a global mission, which make for keen rivalry between the activists. Muslims have viewed the medical and educational work of Christians among them as amounting to a new form of crusade. It seems evident that "some of the most virulent anti-Western nationalists in the Islamic world learned their secular nationalism in . . . missionary schools."[62] The freedom to propagate the Christian message among Muslims is something all Christians would like to enjoy and to have facilitated. The question is whether Christians, respecting freedom of religion, would allow and facilitate a similar call to duty that Muslims may wish to fulfil among them.

Muslims find problematic the rapid changes in Christian self-understanding that is occasioned by secular culture and the propensity to divide, especially in Protestantism. Yet, it is precisely within the context of this secular, plural culture that there exists the necessity for Christian and Muslims to engage each other. Esack rejects the relevance of the Qur'anic notion of "The People of the Book" as a basis for relationship between Muslim and Christians, suggesting that a search for justice is a more appropriate basis for engagement.[63] Muslim-Christian conversation forces us, then, to ask whether Christians, in redefining the meaning of service in the world, will consider Muslims as their partners in the cause of justice.

TAKING STOCK OF THE JOURNEY

We have looked at the background of the Bohemian formula, "in essentials unity, in non-essentials liberty, in all things charity." We saw that this formula, with has antecedence in the pre-reformation era, came to describe a Moravian approach to doctrine and have remained central to Christian self-understanding and piety. We have also looked at aspects of Muslim and Christian self-understanding. We have seen that aspects of Muslim self-understanding, the oneness of God, the

Qur'an as God's final speech and the centrality of the Prophet Muhammad, have implications for the relationship with Christians. Likewise, issues that are fundamental to Christian self-understanding, namely, the place of scripture, the centrality of Jesus and service in the world, have implications for how Muslims view and relate to Christians. We are now in a position to determine what theological conclusions can be drawn from the comparative reflections on aspects of Christian and Muslim self-understanding. How will a Christian account theologically for the faith of the Muslim neighbour? In other words, what can Christians truly say of Islam? In the next chapter we will seek to answer these questions.

NOTES

1. E. De Schweinitz, *The Moravian Manual: Containing an Account of the Moravian Church or Unitas Fratrum* (Bethlehem, PA: A. C. & H. T. Clauder, 1869), 94.

2. Rican, 394.

3. These include the Apostle's, Athanasian, and Nicene Creeds, the 1535 Confession of the Unity of the Bohemian Brethren, the Twenty-One Articles of the Unaltered Augsburg Confession, the shorter Catechism of Martin Luther, the Thirty-Nine Articles of the Church of England, the Theological Declaration of Barmen of 1934 and the Heidelberg Catechism.

4. *Church Order 1995*, 14.

5. F. G. Heymann, *John Zizka and the Hussite Revolution* (Princeton, NJ: Princeton University Press, 1955), 148–149: the *Four Articles of Prague* were the demands laid before the King Sigismund and the representative of the Pope in the Diet of Prague in 1419.

6. Heymann, *John Zizka and the Hussite Revolution*, 148ff.

7. Schweinitz, *The History of the Church*, 202: The three-fold distinction was (1) *credere de Deo*—to believe concerning God, (2) *credere Deo*—to believe God and (3) *credere in Deum*—to believe in God.

8. Schwienitz, *The Moravian Manual*, 95.

9. *The Catechism,* 7.

10. *The Church Book,* 17.

11. F. D. Rees, "The Word in Question: Barth and Divine Conversation" *Pacifica* Vol. 12, #3 (1999): 314.

12. *The Church Book,* 17.

13. *Results of the General Synod of the Brethren's Unity* (London: Moravian Publication, 1881), 10.

14. A. Freeman, "The Hermeneutic of Count Nicholas Ludwig von Zinzendorf," a doctoral dissertation presented to Princeton Seminary, New Jersey, 1962, 242.

15. *Church Order 1995*, 14.

16. P. Avis, "Divine Revelation in Modern Protestant Theology" in P. Avis, Ed., *Divine Revelation* (London: Darton Longman Todd, 1987), 45. The June 26, 1908 is-

sue of *Herrnhut,* a Moravian magazine noted that the lay people feared that the new theology meant "the Savior and Scripture were no longer of value." See Crews, 17.

17. *Church Order 1995,* 14.

18. Schweinitz, *Moravian Manual,* 98.

19. E. Flesseman-van Leer, Ed., *The Bible and Its Authority and Interpretation in the Ecumenical Movement,* (Geneva: WCC, 1980), 13–14.

20. G. O Maynard, *The Moravian Church Among the Churches: Pioneer in the Oecumenical Task* (Barbados: Cedar Press, 1982), 60.

21. A. Schultze, *Christian Doctrine,* 19. Schneiders opines that the notion of inerrancy/infallibility leads to the conception of a God who is authoritarian, who compels rather than invites. Such a conception of God is never found in Moravian piety. See S. Schneiders, *The Revelatory Text: Interpreting the New Testament as Sacred Scripture* (Collegeville, MN: The Liturgical Press, 1999), 55. The 1955 thesis entitled "The Theology of James Montgomery," presented by Lewis Swain to Moravian Theological Seminary, deals with the conception of God in Moravian piety. See especially pp. 15–24, which deals with the doctrine of God.

22. F. Whaling. "Scripture and Its Meanings: A Comparative Perspective Scripture as Texts—Or More," *Studies in World Christianity,* Vol. 6.1 (2000), 80.

23. F. Whaling. "Scripture and Its Meanings, 80.

24. F. Esack, "Muslims Engaging the Other and the Humanum" in J. Witte Jr., R. C. Martin, Eds., *Sharing the Book: Religious Perspectives on the Rights and Wrongs of Proselytism* (Maryknoll, NY: Orbis Books, 1999), 127.

25. Erb, *Pietists,* 3–4. Erb constructs a trajectory from Hus, to Luther, through Arndt to Spener (See, Arndt, *True Christianity,* trans Peter Erb (Toronto, New York: Paulist Press, 1979), xiii.

26. Johann Arndt, *True Christianity,* trans. Peter Erb (Toronto, New York: Paulist Press, 1979), 22.

27. Gambold, *Maxims,* 9.

28. *Church Dogmatics,* II.2 (Edinburgh: T & T Clark, 1957), 568.

29. Barth, *Church Dogmatics: The Doctrine of God,* Vol. II, 1a, 3

30. *Church Dogmatics,* IV.1 (Edinburgh: T & T Clarke, 1956), 683.

31. The christocentric focus of Zinzendorf, however, should be understood in the broader context of his "modest" approach to theology. See Livingstone Thompson, "Harmony, Modesty, Dialogue: A Moravian Contribution Towards the Development of Christian Theologies of Pluralism," (An Unpublished PhD Dissertation Presented to the University of Dublin, May 2003), 196–223.

32. Schweinitz, *The History of the Church,* 202.

33. Schweinitz, *The History of the Church,* 203.

34. *The Catechism,* 10.

35. *The Moravian Hymn Book with Services* (London: Oxford University Press, 1960) # 158.

36. *The Moravian Hymn Book,* # 210.

37. *The Moravian Hymn Book,* # 225.

38. Freeman, "Zinzendorf," 96.

39. Freeman, p. 70.

40. H. Rimius, *A Candid Narrative of the Rise and Progress of the Herrnhutters Commonly called Moravians or Unitas Fratrum: With a Short Account of Their Doctrines, Drawn From Their Own Writings* (London: A. Linde, 1753), 38.

41. C. Atwood, "Blood, Sex, and Death: Life and Liturgy in Zinzendorf's Bethlehem," a doctoral dissertation presented to Princeton Seminary, 1995, 70.

42. Atwood, "Blood, Sex, Death," 67–68.

43. Kinkel, "Count Zinzendorf's Doctrine of the Holy Spirit as Mother," doctoral dissertation submitted to the University of Iowa, 1988, 193. On this question Rahner insists that there is only one hypostatic union, that of the Logos. Yet the Logos is not merely one member of the Godhead who might have revealed to us the true God. See K. Rahner, *The Trinity* (Kent: Burns & Coats, 1970), 25, 30.

44. Kinkel, "Count Zinzendorf," 200. This idea is similar to Rahner's who holds that through the doctrine of the incarnation the Trinity is present everywhere in the life of Jesus. The fact that the Father's word has entered history means that the doctrine of mission is the starting point of what we know of the Trinity. See K. Rahner, *The Trinity*, p. 11 and p. 48.

45. Kinkel, "Count Zinzendorf," 200. We saw above also that early Muslims thought of the the Virgin Mary as Mother beside God the Father and Jesus the Son.

46. *Moravian Manual*, 96. See also *The Book of Order 1911*, 15.

47. *The Church Book*, 18.

48. Blanford, 125. This is a uique interpretation of the formula.

49. Kung, *Christianity and the World Religions*, 107.

50. P. Knitter, *No Other Name? A Critical Survey of Christian Attitudes Towards the World Religions*, 192. Knitter argues for the possibility of multiple incarnations. See also R. Haight, *Jesus Symbol of God* (Maryknoll, NY: Orbis Books, 1999), 456. Haight argues that Spirit Christology removes the need for Jesus to be seen as constitutive for salvation universally.

51. B. Stubenrauch, "Controversy about the Incarnation: What is Specific to Christianity?" *Irish Theological Quarterly* Vol. 64/4 (1999): 351.

52. B. Stubenrauch, "Controversy about the Incarnation, 351.

53. *Issues in Christian-Muslim Relations: Ecumenical Considerations* (WCC Publications: Geneva, 1992), 13.

54. *Church Order 1995*, 13 and16.

55. *Missionary Manual and Directory of the Unitas Fratrum* (Bethlehem, PA: SPGAH, 1875), 2.

56. Hasse, "Consider the Days of Old," 76.

57. *1787–1887 Centennial Anniversary of the Society of the United Brethren for the Propagation of the Gospel Among the Heathen*, November 1, 1887, 35.

58. *Proceedings of the Society for the Propagating of the Gospel to the Heathen: Annual Meeting and Report of the Board of Directors*, (1925): 104.

59. *Proceedings*, (1927): 122–123.

60. *Proceedings*, (1928): 203.

61. Schweinitz, *The History of the Church*, 207.

62. S. H. Nasr, "Islamic Christian Dialogue: Problems and Obstacles to be Pondered and Overcome" *Islam and Christian-Muslim Relations* Vol. 11 (2000): 222.

63. Esack, "Muslims Engaging the Other," 128.

Chapter Six

Speaking of Islam:
What Can Christians Truly Say

SPEAKING THE SAME LANGUAGE?

A fundamental position taken in this study is that the Bohemian formula, "in essentials, unity; in non-essentials, liberty; in all things, charity," is a useful way to construe doctrine for conversation in an interfaith situation. The helpfulness of the formula can be justified on two bases. In the first place, it represents an accepted description of Christian self-understanding, as illustrated, for example, in the Moravian Church. In this approach a distinction is made between things about which absolute claims can be made (essentials) and those things (non-essentials) in which differences must be allowed. This approach to Christian doctrine, which the Moravian Church has preserved for the whole Christian community, finds resonance in the way Muslims understand their faith. Secondly, the notion of hierarchy of truths, which is contained in the formula, is a means whereby the faith may be expressed in different cultures, in a manner that does not result in the separation of Christian truths from its foundation. In other words, the formula recognizes the cultural, contextual, and language limitations of theological discourse. Theological formulations must not be seen as unchangeable descriptions of truth.

In the chapters above we gave an outline of fundamental aspects of the Christian and Muslim faiths. Our task now is to see how the Bohemian formula can help Christians to make statements about Islam that Muslims can accept and which at the same time do not threaten the integrity of the Christian faith. The dialogue between Christians and Muslims that has taken place within the context of the ecumenical movement has demonstrated that there are several areas of convergence between Christians and Muslims:

> Both understand God as Creator and Sustainer, as Just and Merciful, as a God who reveals his word and will call people to account for their stewardship over creation. Both communities of faith stress the centrality of prayer, and share common values and ideals such as the search for justice in society, providing for people in need, love for one's neighbour and living together in peace.[1]

Our aim in this section is to see what else, on the basis of the Bohemian Formula, "in essentials unity," we can affirm about Christians and Muslims. The question we want to answer is whether it is possible for Christians and Muslims to be united in any fundamental aspect of doctrine or self-understanding.

Both Muslim and Christian scholars doubt whether there can be accord between Islam and Christianity. For example the Muslim scholar, Sayyed Hossein Nasr, notes that complete accord between the two religions is not possible in the human atmosphere "but only in the divine stratosphere."[2] In a similar vein, the Christian scholar William Watt believes that it is unlikely that the views of liberal Muslims, who are looking at Christianity afresh, will have any effect on the mainstream of Sunnite or even Shiite Islam.[3] Nevertheless, Nasr sees harmony between the two religions at the metaphysical and the esoteric levels, despite the fact that basic theological issues remain unresolved on the formal theological level.[4] This theological stalemate is derived, at least in part, from the fact that the starting point of theological discourse has tended to be revealed truth (or revelation), whether as contained in the Qur'an, or as witnessed to in the Bible. The doctrine of divine revelation is concerned with "how . . . self-transcending revelatory disclosure is possible."[5] The problem for interfaith dialogue between Muslims and Christians, however, is not the different conclusions arrived at in the religious traditions, but the *a priori* assumptions about the source or sources of revealed truth.[6] For example, Christians believe in a God who has a loving nature, "presupposed by the existence of material beings [i.e. humans] capable of loving self-transcendence,"[7] yet God is still unknowable. This movement from human experience to absolute claims about God as ultimate reality is logically unjustified. Consequently, given the challenge of interfaith dialogue, there is the need to investigate a different starting point for theology, one that believers of different religious traditions may take without colliding in their discourse; one that is able to maintain the weight of the theological superstructures. We need a discourse that is characterized by modesty in the assertions that are made about God; a discourse in which account is taken that language about God is not precise science and what we believe in not the product of empirical evidence. We need a discourse in which there is recognition of the limits of human capacity to know absolute, divine reality.

TOWARDS A THEOLOGY OF MODESTY

The theologian Nicholas *von* Zinzendorf offers us some help in moving towards the delineation of a discourse that is characterized by the modesty of which we speak. The theology of modesty, of which we speak here, is a theological discourse that takes place with a keen awareness of the limits of human knowledge of the divine life, notwithstanding any assertion about revelation in Christ of the Qur'an. Two major principles govern this theological discourse. The first is that we should limit the expectations we place on reason to help us grasp divine truths. Overconfidence in the capacity of reason not only leads to a suspicion of biblical truths but also leads to religious arrogance and immodesty in our relationship with others. When reason is exercised without faith and without a sense of its own limitation it often leads to confusion.[8] Zinzendorf illustrated this with reference to the reading of the Christian scriptures. He argued that when the reader endeavors to situate himself/herself within the world of Holy Scripture and tries to speak from that perspective it would be difficult for that reader to doubt the incarnation, the divinity of Christ and the redemption of souls, unless the reader is "possessed of a confused understanding, or a knavish heart."[9] Either that person sees more than he is willing to allow or with conceit and immodesty claims to see farther than his insight really reaches. In these comments he was making a critique of emerging approaches to scriptural interpretation, for example deism and the historical critical method, which seemed to require the reader to let go of some of the fundamental truths of the Christian faith. Zinzendorf's approach, therefore, is usually read only as a conservation reaction to the Enlightenment's attack on revealed religion.[10] However, Zinzendorf recognized reason as a God-given capacity but limited its role in matters of faith. In so doing, he was putting forward an epistemology that was designed to undercut the claims to certitude in the sphere of metaphysics. In this way Zinzendorf was preempting the post-modern period which is suspicious of claims to certitude and objectivity.

The critique of certitude in metaphysics was a task that Kant would later take up, though not from the same point of view. Zinzendorf's limitation of reason, which preceded Kant's philosophical critique, was from a theological point of view. According to Zinzendorf, the understanding of the human being in divine matters is analogous to that of a poor animal in the comprehension of geometric or algebraic propositions. His approach, then, was to concede limitations to reason in dealing with some matters that he felt could only be appreciated from the perspective religious faith. He said he would use reason in human matters so far as it sufficed, but in spiritual matters he remained simply with the heart-grasped truth, which little children could understand. These little scholars of the Holy Ghost, as he called children, "get acquainted

with their Abba and their divine Mother too [i.e. the Holy Spirit] at the same
time, as soon as they are capable of thinking."[11] As far as it relates to God
Zinzendorf believed we were to say, "I am Behema, a dumb animal before
[God]; I cannot penetrate into the depths of things."[12] This modesty in what
the human being can say about God implies that we should be less assertive
about our claims to knowledge of God. Over-confidence in the role of reason,
therefore, will have negative consequences for the understanding and faith of
individuals.

The second principle that governs the theology of modesty we see in
Zinzendorf is the linking of modesty and ignorance godliness. This is a revo-
lutionary thought in a context and an age that evidences a kind of Gnosticism.
We see this, for example, in the thinking that correct knowledge is a prerequisite for salvation and that only a certain group of people have access to this
knowledge. The move to point out the limits of human reason in Zinzendorf's
theology of modesty was based on his interpretation of the story of Adam and
Eve in Genesis 3. He argued that ignorance is God's way to keep mortals
from being dried up by the same satanic spirit of rebellion that was evidenced
in the Garden of Eden. In keeping the human being close to the beast in regard to knowledge, God was thwarting Satan's scheme, which was designed
to make human beings like God through the faculty of reason.[13] Although this
faculty is God-given, it was the main instrument of Satan's scheme against
God. Those people, therefore, who are keen to exercise themselves in knowledge and to show the greatness of their reasoning abilities in matters of faith
are in fact co-operating with Satan. According to Zinzendorf, the fall does not
consist in the lust of the flesh but in the lust of the mind, a seeking to know
where one should be keen to love. God's conversation with Adam was in effect a critique of those who were more concerned with insight and reflection
than with love.[14] For Zinzendorf, there was then no need to represent Christianity as being agreeable with common sense. As soon as an attempt was
made "to demonstrate to atheists and common deists and people like that that
our religion is a wisdom rooted in their heads, a discernment which they can
take in their own way, then they are obviously threshing empty straw."[15] On
the contrary, the means of understanding available to the human being is not
sufficient for the Christian message. We should then not be surprised, indeed
it is to be expected that Christianity will be treated as foolishness.

By recognizing the spiritual value of ignorance, Zinzendorf can be situated
at the outskirts of the apophatic tradition where there is preparedness to
negate assertions about God, in order to underline the limits of human language and mental formulations. The interfaith significance of this approach is
that it provides space for dialogue with people of other faiths who are ignorant of Christian claims and who, for many Christians, are ignorant of God.

When Christians take this approach in the encounter with people of other religions, the outcome cannot be known in advance. Openness to the future and
to God, which is a consequence of theological modesty, means that in we cannot predict what will happen to us or people of other faiths because God could
surprise us.[16]

THE INTERFAITH IMPLICATIONS
OF THEOLOGICAL MODESTY

When Zinzendorf is read closely there seem to emerge at least three emphases in his theological modesty that have implications for pluralism. The
first is the apophatic-like character of his theology, a tension between what
he knows about God and what he does not know; between what he sees and
what cannot be seen; between what he experiences and what is beyond experience; between what he speaks of and that for which he has no appropriate language. The consequence of this tension in his thought is a refusal to
treat theological assertions with any kind of dogmatic finality but to regard
them as provisional. The Moravian *Church Order* captures this idea with its
statement that: "The Unitas Fratrum maintains that all creeds formulated by
the Christian Church stand in need of constant testing in the light of the Holy
Scriptures."[17] As in negative theology, Zinzendorf doubts the capacity of the
human mind to be able to formulate permanent assertions about God, of
whom we only form glimpses through the Incarnate One. To focus on theological modesty, then, is to perform a hermeneutical act of retrieval not only
of Zinzendorf but also of the apophatic tradition, which is a credible approach to doing theology.[18] At the centre of the retrieved discourse is the idea
that our language, which deals with things within human experience, cannot
properly apply to God since God cannot be contained within the categories
of human experience.

The second aspect of Zinzendorf's theological modesty that emerges on
close reading is a human-centred Christology. Zinzendorf emphasised Jesus
as a historical figure and refused to be drawn into speculation about his divinity. However, he maintained a traditional understanding of the mystery of
the hypostatic union—that all the time the man Jesus was God. In order to
bring the modesty of the Creator into sharp focus, Zinzendorf takes pain to
underline the human-like-us character of Jesus. He stressed that in his incarnation Jesus himself was not always aware of his divinity because of the reality of his human consciousness. This means Jesus had limitations of mem-
ory, of vision and of knowledge.[19] Zinzendorf sees the recovery of the history
of the man Jesus as a most urgent theological task.

The third issue that Zinzendorf's theological modesty seems to involve is a perspective of openness to the future, which we might call surprise eschatology. This is the sense in which he discusses theological issues relating to soteriology, and the mission of the church. The human mind, he argues, cannot fathom the fullness of God's activity in the world and so we do not know what God may be doing among people who do not yet believe in Jesus. The mystery of God's salvation is not about the unsaved but about those who are saved, for we do not know why the Holy Spirit has called those who are called. A further surprise awaits us as we journey towards the immense God because even after a hundred aeons in eternity we will not yet arrive to the one to whom we are flying. So the future is open, which means its nature will come as a surprise to believers as well as for the non-believers.

As a result of the limits he placed on reason, Zinzendorf was keen to avoid the danger of approaching Christian truths as if they can be known before they are believed. He therefore does not put the need to understand doctrines as a primary Christian task. He considers it an ancient rule of the Christian church that articles of faith are to be overlooked at the first introduction in the faith.[20] Zinzendorf therefore objected to the practice where verbal assent to doctrines in the confession of creeds was used as a means to determine one's religious status.[21] For him, the proof of knowledge of the truth was not verbal assent but the preparedness to suffer for the truth. The person, then, to whom the truths of the faith were not preached should not be expected either to believe them or to suffer as a consequence of not understanding them.

For Zinzendorf, it is the Holy Spirit in its operation as teacher that enables someone to understand the doctrines of the faith that must be first believed. The Holy Spirit, he argued, engaged with individuals depending on their level of knowledge. It was not necessary, according to him, for people of have the same level of knowledge to have access to the eternal life. In fact, their eternal bliss was not a consequence of their knowledge because: whether one "afterwards go to heaven out of the fifth, fourth, third, or the first class or a select class, still he has the very same happiness."[22] He further cautioned us about having unreasonable or unrealistic expectations about the extent of human awareness of God. The wise student of the Holy Spirit would not attempt to treat things of a higher class than where he or she is located. Heresy and the judgment of having a weak mind arise when one is so presumptuous as to attempt to enter upon the things of a higher class.

To insist that people understand doctrine in order to believe was for Zinzendorf an attempt to subvert the normal mode of operation of the Holy Spirit. Upon believing, the Holy Spirit will teach us the things we need to know but an inquisitive attitude is at variance with the modesty and presumption of ignorance that is suited for holiness. In order then that the truths of the Christian faith be understood, it would be necessary first to have everlasting life, which consists in the simple knowledge that the death of Jesus was a saving death.[23]

There is, obviously, no scope within this present study to fully develop these principles. What is critical here for our argument is the recognition that ignorance is seen as a common human condition and is amenable to theological discourse. The admittance of ignorance of the divine life is a point at which there is unity between the religious traditions. A theology of modesty is based on the presumption of ignorance of the divine life and is therefore compatible with Christian theology. However, it is still to be seen whether there is a similar conception of ignorance in Islam, which may lead to a common affirmation between Christians and Muslims.

THEOLOGICAL MODESTY IN THE QUR'AN

The Qur'an is replete with references to things that may or may not be known. For example, Surah 32 deals extensively with the mysteries of creation, time and the final end (*Ma'ad*). The contemplation of these things "should lead to faith and the adoration of Allah,"[24] because a full grasp of them is never possible. In Surah 31:34 we find reference to the absolute knowledge of Allah:

> Verily the knowledge of the Hour is with Allah (alone). It is He who sends down rain, and He Who knows what is in the wombs. Nor does anyone know what it is that he will earn on the morrow; nor does anyone know in what land he is to die. Verily with Allah is full knowledge and he is acquainted (with all things).[25]

In commenting on this verse, 'Abdullah Yusuh 'Ali notes that the knowledge that human beings possess, amounts only to a "superficial acquaintance with things."[26] While there is no uncertainty about absolute truth, "as received by men, and understood in reference to men's psychology, certainty may have certain degrees."[27] In fact, truth may be divided in three categories: *'ilm al yaqin*, certainty that arises from appraisal of evidence (juridical truth); *'ain al yaqin*, certainty by personal inspection (empirical truth); and *haqq al yaqin*, absolute truth.[28] When it comes to the question of absolute truth, humanity must confess ignorance because it is a prerogative of God alone. As Dupuis notes, divine mystery remains irremediably beyond human grasp.[29] Moreover, "no religious tradition can, *a priori*, claim a privileged knowledge of the Divine Mystery, let alone a monopoly of knowledge."[30]

The presumption of ignorance may provide a resolution to the concerns about the Prophethood of Muhammad that we find among Christians. As noted earlier, Christians are reluctant to regard him as a prophet, on account of the content of the revelation he brought. However, Muslims believe that the authenticity of his Prophethood is indicated first of all by the fact that he was *ummi*, which means illiterate (Surah 7:157).[31] Muhammad was believed to have been unable to read or write, so that he was a clean vessel to receive the revelation he was told to recite. In fact, this presumption of ignorance, according to Surah 62:2,[32] was a condition of the whole people to whom the Prophet was sent. Although this condition of *ummi* in the Prophet may be a backward mythic projection (similar to the infancy narratives of Jesus), it provides a basis, prior to the revelation, for considering the question of the authenticity of the Prophet. If Christians can see that as *ummi*, Muhammad was an ideal vessel for the receipt of revelation, there is then no need to begin with the content of the revelation when seeking to authenticate his Prophethood. His role as a prophet is predicated on character as *ummi*, which made him an ideal vessel for the revelations.

Muslims and Christian can, then, agree with Dupuis that, "all human knowledge of the Absolute is relative."[33] Despite the revelations in the Qur'an and those to which the Bible bear witness, human knowledge of God remains imperfect and fragmentary. Although God chose "to have a difference remain[ing] between the knowledge of his children,"[34] this, for Zinzendorf, did not make null and void the fundamental notion of ignorance. As far as he was concerned, imperfect and fragmentary knowledge amounts to ignorance. This lack of knowledge is the state of affairs that provided the restraint in making absolute claims.

Returning then to the theology of modesty, we may say that Christians and Muslims can together affirm that humanity is fundamentally ignorant of absolute truth, the revelation of which creates degrees of uncertainty and relativity in the human community. The full knowledge of the divine life belongs to the category of absolute truth, an awareness that neither Moravians nor Muslims can claim. Put another way, neither of the two traditions can attempt to claim the higher epistemological ground because they stand together on the same ground of human ignorance. Human ignorance, then, is a common point at which Muslims and Christians can begin their theological discourse. It is on this basis that Christians and Muslims can affirm, "in ignorance, unity," because both communities desire to come to a fuller knowledge of God's will.

The genius of the approach that is predicated on the presumption of ignorance is that partners in conversation are modest in the claims about what they know. This is a particularly important approach, especially for those who are engaged in interfaith dialogue.

IN IGNORANCE—UNITY

It would seem that both Christians and Muslims agree that despite what they know about God, from the revelation of Jesus in the Bible and from the revelation in the Qur'an, there is still a considerable level of ignorance about the divine life and the divine will. In other words, neither Christians nor Muslims can claim to know God to the extent it can be said there is nothing further that needs to be known. This concession of ignorance about God is something that adherents of both religious communities can affirm together. We can say, then, that at the starting point of any religious conversation between Christians and Muslims that there is a presumption of ignorance concerning the Almighty Creator.

Note should be taken of churches, which are prepared to admit their limited knowledge of God. The Church Order of the Moravian Church, for example, states that there is a mystery about God and God's will, which even though witnessed to in scripture, "cannot be comprehended completely by any human mind or expressed completely in any human statement."[35] It is this idea of ignorance that was the basis of the unwillingness of the renewed Moravian Church to develop any doctrinal statement of its own. This unwillingness to encase revelation in fixed theological formulas, or to claim complete certainty in knowledge about divine reality was clearly articulated by Zinzendorf in two classical discourses; (1) Lecture VII of the *Nine Public Lectures on Important Subjects in Religion*, entitled "On the essential Character and Circumstances of the Life of a Christian" and (2) Discourse X of the *Twenty-One Discourses or Dissertation upon the Augsburg-Confession*. Arguing for the "foolishness of the gospel," as in 1Cor 1: 18, Zinzendorf begged theologians, "not to take such pains constantly to represent our religion as agreeing with reason, as being common sense."[36] There is no understanding sufficient enough to penetrate the matters of the faith. The understanding of a human being "is as insufficient for grasping our matters [of faith]."[37] As the Psalmist, we should to say, "I am Behema, a dumb animal before [God]; I cannot penetrate into the depths of things."[38]

Zinzendorf refused to speculate about subjects like the Trinity, the redemption of the devils and the eternal hope of those who turn their backs on God. Since there was no certain knowledge of those matters in Scripture, and since, in any case, they belong to the mysterious and obscure, "we ought to leave [them] to God Almighty, . . . nor ought we . . . to furnish the least opportunity of leading people into points of knowledge *praeter Scripturam*."[39] Indulgence in matters of which there is no certainty, "mingles the children of God in matters foreign to them and thwarts the Saviour's etiquette and entire regulation with his own."[40] Speculation into subjects like the restoration of devils or the thousand-year reign (the latter mentioned in the Book of Revelation), is "entirely incompatible with heart-principles, and with the daily inculcating of the person and merits of our Saviour."[41] When faced with the uncertainty of things, the best that can be done is to focus on the principles that are certain, leaving God to reveal the rest to us. For this eighteenth century pietist, acquired knowledge does not allow human beings to get closer to the mind of God.[42]

The unwillingness to make absolute claims about knowledge of divine things is reflected in the litanies of the Moravian Church, which include a prayer that Christians, like Islam, "may come to a fuller knowledge of [God's] truth and love."[43] This caution in making claims about knowledge and the preference for being considered as ignorant and foolish, because speculation was seen as a hindrance rather than a help to the heart's acceptance of truth, is one of the reasons behind the paucity of systematic theological material within the Moravian tradition. However, this caution now provides a basis on which to develop a theological position, within which people of other faiths, beginning with Islam, can find a point of departure for their own discourse in a plural context.

The argument being advanced here is that admitting ignorance of God or theological modesty, is a starting point for theological discussion that is more amenable to inter-faith conversation than using notions of revelation.[44]

IN FAITH–PROXIMITY

To say that Christians and Muslims are at one in their desire to know more fully the will of God is not all that Christians can say. If we take the case of the Moravian Church, one can discern within it a mixture of perceptions of Islam. An oscillation in perception was evident at the 1887 Centennial of the Moravian missions society, the Society for Propagating the Gospel Among the Heathen. On one hand, Muhammad is referred to as a "false prophet,"[45] while on the other hand, Islam was not counted among the heathens, nor was it seen as an object of evangelism. The conference noted, that at the last decade of the nineteenth century, there were three and a half times as many Christians as there were Muslims in the world. The pagans, who were the object of missionary efforts, were more than all the Christians, Jews and Muslims put together. To focus of the missionary endeavor should be on those who have not yet come to faith rather than on those who were of a different religious faith.[46]

The most significant encounters between Moravians and people of other faiths have taken place in Africa, Tibet Surinam, the Middle East and Guyana. The analyses of the experiences in these locations also reveal somewhat contradictory perceptions of Islam. In Tanzania, for example, Islam was seen as a threat to Moravian ministry. A report, dated 1926, classed the Muslims as having moral standards that were "not above but rather below those of the heathen."[47] In was in that very year Muslims were accused of setting fire to a

Moravian Church. While the relationship between the two groups in this lo-cation has moved from antagonism to mutual respect, Moravians in Africa, unlike other areas, continue to see Muslims as objects of their evangelistic ef-forts.[48] Similarly, in a 1927 report from Tibet, mention is made of "minds and hearts seared and hardened by either Buddhism or Mohammedanism."[49] In the same negative vein, reports out of Surinam in 1943 and 1944 treated Is-lam as a special case of heathenism because of its "meticulous legalism" and the fact that "it took over much from [Judaism] and Christianity."[50]

For the most part, the reports out of Jerusalem and a perspective from Guyana indicate an opposite tone. While the Muslims were chided for their legalism and stubbornness, they were the main recipients of the loving care of the medical staff of the leper home in Jerusalem. The motive of the Jerusalem mission was not evangelization, but "Christlike service [by] the nurses, who learn and teach the love that beareth all things, believeth all things, hopeth all things, and which never faileth."[51] In the leper home, the medical staff respected the piety of the Muslims because they always showed interest in the pastoral addresses of the Christian chaplains. The Home was a community of mainly Muslims and Christians, who agreed that, "whatever may take place outside [the] Home, . . . [they] remain[ed] faithful friends."[52] As was the case in Surinam, the Home had the practice of reading from the Bible and the Qur'an at community gatherings. Writing with the benefit of the experiences of Muslims in Guyana, George Richmond, then Chairman of the Provincial Board of the Moravian Church concludes:

> Islam with its monotheistic focus and stress on themes of prayer, mercy and charity, has a natural bonding with Christianity. Further, Islam's unification of the sacred and the secular in Muslim countries should be a reminder to Chris-tians of the need to have our faith permeate all aspects of daily living.[53]

The experiences of the missionaries may have influenced the insertion of the statement that, " God shows no partiality to race or culture [and] all who have reverence for him and do what is right are acceptable to God,"[54] in the Litany for World Mission. The further maturing of the perception of Islam is probably best indicated by the account of a Moravian who married into a Muslim family:

> As an American Moravian living in a Moslem community in East Jerusalem, I have always felt at home. I grew up in Nazareth, Pennsylvania, with much time spent in the church and in close access to the Whitefield tract, where I had first had exposure to dedicated Moravian missionaries. . . . What I learned from them definitely prepared me for my life in East Jerusalem and the loving Muslim fam-ily and community who made me feel at home.[55]

The significance of this account is that it comes not from a theologian, but from a rank and file member of the church, which confirms what is affirmed in the Moravian Book of worship, which boldly asserts that Islam is "close to [Christianity] in heritage and faith."[56] Although no justification is given for this assertion, analysis of Moravian perceptions of Islam in earlier years accord with this assessment. For example, in the writings of the eighteenth century Moravian theologian, Zinzendorf, there was also the recognition that Muslims, like Jews, believe that there is one God, even though they excluded Jesus or denied his true form and nature.[57] The views of the leaders of the church seemed to have weigh heavily on 1995 assertion in the Book of Worship. It is probably accurate, therefore, to say that the Moravian perception of Islam is such that Christians can say of Islam, "in faith, proximity."

From the point of view of the whole Christian community, the most important challenge to take Islam seriously was already recognized in the writings of the seventeenth century irenic Christian philosopher, Comenius. He believed that all religions having a claim for a book with a divine status must bring them into the public arena for common reading. The disclosive authority of scripture emerges in dialogical rather than in unilateral reading. The effect of the Comenian approach is to incline people living in a plural context to practice multiple reading of scriptures. In his view, it is not acceptable for Christians to pass judgement on the Qur'an without having read it with the intention of finding where it is in harmony with the Christian Bible and in harmony with sense and reason. More critically, since there is the claim that the Qur'an is of divine origin, it is incumbent on the Christian to read those scriptures in a similar way as the Bible is read as a prelude to passing judgement on its content. To immediately reject the claim that others have a book from God, though different from our own, is to run the risk of refusing to listen to the voice of God. Refusing to listen to what God is believed by others to have said:

> Imposes blindness upon God. In other words, he imagines God as a blind, deaf, and dumb idol or a cruel tyrant who perhaps watches our downfall and destruction with a smile of indifference and certainly does not intervene as He might. Since no one could wish for such an absurd God, the idea would be unthinkable, and when one hears that books are being circulated in God's name, one would wish them to be truly divine so that we may listen to God. This is the first point on which we must agree, that some books must exist in which the voice of God himself is recorded, no matter how far we have to go to find them.[58]

The assertion of Comenius can lead Christians to say of Islam, as is affirmed in the Moravian worship book, that Islam is close to Christians in faith: in others words, we are proximate in faith.

If Christians are at one with Muslims in the limits if their know of the divine life and if Christians are proximate to Islam in faith, what do we do with the revelation of Jesus. Our final task, then, is to deal with the issue of Christology, which, many will attest, is one of the more problematic issues in interfaith dialogue. Will Christians continue to insist that there is only one credible perception of Christ? What sorts of differences are allowable in Christology? In so far as we challenge Muslims to re-think the perception they have of the Qur'an, then overcoming the conflicts in Christian-Muslim conversation imply that we must also face these question about Christology. We turn now to consider these issues.

IN CHRISTOLOGY–DIFFERENCE

It is impossible to bypass the issue of Christology when Christians are involved in interfaith dialogue. For the dialogue between Muslims and Christians it is a necessary consideration, not only because there is a special place accorded to Jesus in the Qur'an, but, more so, because it is not possible to have a full understanding of Christianity with the incarnation bracketed out. Responding to the view that Christian uniqueness should be softened, Dupuis asserts: "the Christian faith cannot stand without claiming for Jesus Christ a constitutive uniqueness."[59]

When we read Christian history, however, we find that there are different accounts of how we might understand and speak of Jesus. These differences in Christology have emerged because of that uniqueness and the centrality of Christ for Christians. As there have been differences in ecclesiology, so there have been differences in Christology. In a 1963 address to the WCC Fourth World Conference on Faith and Order, Ernst Kasemann dispensed with the conception of unity in New Testament ecclesiology. He notes:

> The tensions between Jewish Christian and Gentile Christian churches, between Paul and the Corinthian enthusiasts, between John and early Catholicism are as great as those of our day. Onesided emphases, fossilized attitudes, fabrications and contradictory opposites in doctrine, organization and devotional practice are to be found in the ecclesiology of the New Testament no less than among ourselves.[60]

Writing in the same vein, Knitter notes that from the very beginning Christology was diverse and the result of dialogue. Relying on Schillebeeckx, Knitter argues for four trajectories in Christology, namely, the Maranatha, the Divine Man, the Logos, and the Paschal.[61] With the conviction that all christologies are culturally situated, Roger Haight has recently outlined seven approaches to

Christology that he finds evident today. These he describes as, the Transcendental Christology, Narrative Christology, Existential Christology, Liberation Christology, Feminist Christology, Inculturated Christology and Process Christology.[62] These contemporary christologies take their bearing from the New Testament christologies seen in Paul, in Mark, in Luke and in John.[63] However, neither the New Testament, nor "a correlation between scripture and common human experience that bypasses or jumps over intervening history,"[64] is sufficient for christology. The christological language of any period "is a continuation of its immediate and longer-term past."[65]

If christology continued to develop after the New Testament, then it would seem that the only constant feature of christology is its propensity to develop in several directions. It should therefore not be surprising that Islam, with a developed tradition of reflection on the work of Jesus, articulated a different christology from what has been emphasized in the orthodox Christian tradition.[66] With the seminal work of Geoffrey Parrinder, *Jesus in the Qur'an*, it is not necessary to make a case for a qur'anic christology. The name of Jesus, together with the titles Son of Mary (*Ibn Maryam*), Messiah (*Masih*), Word (*kalima*) and Spirit (*ruh*), is mentioned several times in the Qur'an. While these terms are also used of Jesus in the Bible, we should not assume that they play the same role in Muslim piety as they do in Christianity. Referring particularly to the title Word (*kalima*), van Ess noted that, "it . . . lost for Muhammad the implication it once had for the Greeks and . . . for Christians today."[67] The simple fact is that the picture of Jesus in the Qur'an does not accord with the picture of Jesus in the Bible nor with the greater emphases in the Christian tradition, an observation that Muslims scholars readily concede.[68] An example of this difference is Jesus' divinity, which Christians affirm but which Muslims deny. What then is the consequence of these different perceptions? Can Christians live with the differences?

The fact is that Christians are already living with different perceptions of Jesus. There are those who find that the christological language of the early church cannot mediate the meaning in today's context that it evidently conveyed in an earlier period. They are, therefore, seeking new christological formulations because christological formulations can no longer be treated as timeless "essentials." Like the creeds, christological formulations are human cultural formulas and should not be treated as statements of absolute truth. They suffer from cultural, contextual and language limitations. The end result of the new formulations is a new perception of Christ. Moreover, the existence of conflicting positions on christology in one tradition has not torn the tradition apart. For example, the theologians Dupuis and Knitter are both from the Roman Catholic Church but they have different perceptions of Jesus—the former would regard himself as an inclusivist and the latter as a pluralist. These different views have not been disallowed. This can only be taken to mean that, in christology, differences must be allowed because of the very nature of the subject. If difference can be tolerated within one tradition, then there is no reason to suppose that it cannot be tolerated between two different traditions. Christians do not have to accept or be threatened by the christology of the Qur'an, nor should there be any attempt to harmonize it with their own. Qur'anic christology is consistent with but not fundamental to the self-understanding of Islam. Changes in qur'anic christology should be expected to arise only from changes in those things that are fundamental to Muslim self-understanding. By the same token, Moravian christology is consistent with Moravian self-understanding and is different from the christology of the Qur'an. At the end of the day, Christians and Muslims will have to confess, "in christology, difference." In other words, both communities have different perceptions of Jesus, which are linked to their own religious histories. Christians believe that the account of Jesus that we find in the Bible is more accurate than that which is found in the Muslim scripture. However, it is not possible to re-write the Qur'an in light of the discrepancies. Rather, we have to live with them. This is not a life threatening position and, given the particularities of contexts and the limitations of language, the different perceptions of Christ are understandable and, as some may even say, helpful and necessary.

NOTES

1. *Issues in Christian-Mulim Relations*, 8.
2. S. H. Nasr, "Islamic-Christian Dialogue," 214.
3. Watt, *Muslim-Christian Relations*, 129.
4. Nasr, "Islamic-Christian Dialogue," 215.
5. N. Lossky, et al, Eds., *Dictionary of the Ecumenical Movement* (Geneva: WCC, 1991), 868–869.
6. For example, some concepts of ultimate reality are monotheistic others are not. See K. E. Yandell, *Philosophy of Religion: A Contemporary Introduction* (London and New York: Routledge, 1999), 83–116.
7. Lossky, 869; The Dictionary makes reference here to Karl Rahner's argument.
8. Zinzendorf, *Twenty-One Discourses,* XI, 162; Gambold, *Maxims,*130; Zinzendorf, *Twenty-One Discourses,* VI, 89.
9. Zinzendorf, *Twenty-One Discourses,* VI, 91.
10. Renkewitz, "Zinzendorf als Theologe," 77; Betterman, 11; Freeman, 41.
11. Zinzendorf, *Twenty-One Discourses,* II, 25–26.
12. Zinzendorf, *Nine Public Lectures,* VII, 78.
13. Zinzendorf, *Twenty-One Discourses*, IX, 121.
14. Zinzendorf, *Twenty-One Discourses,* IX, 122–3.
15. Zinzendorf, *Nine Public Lectures* , VII, 78.

16. As the 1996 World Mission Conference of the WCC put it: "on our journey of dialogue Christians—as well as their partners from other religions—may be surprised, for Christ may encounter them where they would never have expected him." [Christopher Duraisingh, ed., *Called to One Hope: The Gospel in Diverse Cultures* (Geneva: WCC, 1998), 61.] In an unexpected way the hermeneutics of modesty is akin to a hermeneutics of suspicion and is strongly eschatological. A hermeneutic of suspicion says, "it is not necessarily so." A hermeneutic of modesty says, "I have not seen any thing as yet." An approach of modesty seems to suggest that we have not seen every thing as yet, or what we have seen may be other than it seems. Cracknell describes an approach like this as the "You Ain't Seen Nothing Yet" approach to the future of religion. [Kenneth Cracknell, "The Theology of Religious Plurality," *Current Dialogue* 26 (June 1994) :16–18.] In discussing the possibilities for the religious future he opts for this approach over against three other possibilities, namely: the ultimate triumph of one religious tradition over all the others; the deliberate creation of a new religion; and the conscious decision by religious communities to continue living in various forms of splendid isolation.

17. *Church Order*, 1,5. "In the light of Holy Scriptures" should be taken here to mean in the light of new interpretations.

18. David Tracy underlines that the theological classics were retrieved from within the Christian tradition; Barth of Calvin; Lonergan and Rahner of Aquinas, Reinhold Niebuhr of Augustine; Richard Niebuhr of Jonathan Edwards; Paul Tillich and Bultmann of Luther. David Tracy, *The Analogical Imagination: Christian Theology and the Culture of Pluralism,* (London: SCM, 1981), 104.

19. Zinzendorf, *Twenty-One Discourses,* V, 75: ." . . [his participation in the Godhead was] concealed from, and became a mystery to him."

20. Zinzendorf, *Sixteen Discourses,* Preface, 3.

21. Zinzendorf, *Twenty-One Discourse*, I, 2.

22. Zinzendorf, *Twenty-One Discourses,* I, 7.

23. Zinzendorf, *Twenty-One Discourses,* 12.

24. *The Holy Qur'an*, 1044; introduction to Surah 32.

25. *The Qur'an*, 1043; "what he will earn tomorrow" is to be understood to mean that which will happen to the individual in the future.

26. *The Holy Qur'an*, 1043.

27. *The Holy Qur'an*, 1523; note 5673; my emphasis.

28. *The Holy Qur'an*, 1523; note 5673.

29. J. Dupuis, *Toward a Christian Theology of Religious Pluralism* (Maryknoll, NY: Orbis Books, 1997), 281.

30. J. Dupuis, *Toward a Christian Theology of Religious Pluralism* (Maryknoll, NY: Orbis Books, 1997), 281.

31. Cragg, *The Event of the Qur'an*, 59, notes that this may also mean "unscriptured."

32. See note 5449 in 'Abdullah Yusaf 'Ali's commentary in *The Meaning of the Holy Qur'an*, 1466.

33. Dupuis shares the view of Swindler that truth is conditioned by history, by context, by language, by interpretation and that truth is dialogical. See Dupuis, 285.

34. *Twenty-One Discourses*, 152.

35. *Moravian Church Order 1995*, 14. Traces of the philosopher Leibniz can be seen in Zinzendorf theology. Like Leibniz before him, Zinzendorf was close to the Prussian aristocracy and had a similar passion for ecumenical philosophy and theology. Leibniz died in 1716, the same year Zinzendorf matriculated at the University of Wittenberg. (See A. Kenny, *A Brief History of Western Philosophy* (Oxford, UK and Malden, MA: Blackwell Publishers, 1998), 224. However, with his emphasis on ignorance, he was also reacting to the critique that the Enlightenment philosophers made on religion. See, G. Kinkel, *It Started with Zinzendorf: A Mission Study Then and Now* (Bethlehem, PA: Moravian Publications Office, 1996), 7–11.

36. G. Forrell, Ed., *Nine Public Lectures on Important Subjects in Religion: Preached in Fetter Lane Chapel in the Year 1746* (Iowa City: University of Iowa Press, 1973), 78.

37. *Nine Public Lectures*, 78.

38. *Nine Public Lectures*, 78.

39. *Twenty-One Discourse or Dissertations upon the Augsburg-Confession*, trans. by F. Okelley (London: W. Bowyer, 1753), 145.

40. *Twenty-One Discourse*, 149.

41. *Twenty-One Discourse*, 151.

42. *Twenty-One Discourse*, 153.

43. *Moravian Book of Worship* (Bethlehem, PA & Winston-Salem, NC: Board of Publications, 1995), 7.

44. Esack does not deal with the issue of ignorance, but recognizes the importance of anthropology as fundamental to interfaith relations. See references to works by Farid Esack in this article. In the article "Muslims Engaging the Other and the Humanum" he asserts, "The Qur'an relates dogma to socioeconomic exploitation and insists on connecting orthodoxy with orthopraxis." (p. 132)

45. *Centennial Anniversary*, 34.

46. *Centennial Anniversary*, 47–48.

47. *Proceedings*, (1926): 116.

48. In letter to this writer, dated June 16, 2000, Chairman of the Provincial Board of the Rungwe Province in Tnanzania writes, "officially, we practice the evangelization of the Moslems."

49. *Proceedings* (1927): 104.

50. *Proceedings* (1943): 114; *Proceedings* (1944): 10.

51. Proceedings (1925): 104; my emphasis.

52. *Proceedings* (1929), 106.

53. G. Richmond, "The Finality of Christ: Is Jesus Christ the Only Way to Salvation?" a thesis presented to Moravian Theological Seminary, 1991, 64; my emphasis.

54. *Moravian Book of Worship*, 68; this is similar to a text in the Qur'an: Surah 16:30: "To those who do good, there is good is this world, and the Home of the hereafter is even better."

55. S. Beitel Jamjoum, "From Pennsylvania to East Jerusalem: Similarities and Differences," *The Moravian*, Vol. 28, No. 4 (1997): 10. Jamjoum uses the two different renderings "Moslem" and "Muslim."

56. *Moravian Book of Worship*, 7.

57. *Sixteen Discourse on Jesus Christ our Lord: Being an Exposition of the Second Part of the Creed*, (London: W. Bowyer, 1750), 3.

58. *Sixteen Discourse on Jesus Christ our Lord*, 3.

59. Dupuis, *Toward a Christian Theology*, p. 304. By "constitutive uniqueness" Dupuis means that Jesus has a universal significance for all humankind. He is a privileged channel through which God has chosen to share the divine life with human beings.

60. M. Kinnamon and B. Cope, Eds., *The Ecumenical Movement: An Anthology of Key Texts and Voices* (Geneva: WCC Publications, 1997), 97.

61. P. Knitter, *No Other Name*, 176 & 177.

62. Haight, *Jesus Symbol of God*, 17ff.

63. Haight, 154.

64. Haight, 213.

65. Haight, 213.

66. van Ess argues, however, that this christology in the Qur'an has similarities in the Christian Tradition. See Kung, 100.

67. Kung, *Christianity and the World Religions*, 99.

68. van Ess is unapologetic for this fact, noting that the same can be said of the Bible in its treatment of John the Baptist. See Kung, 99.

Conclusion

The aim of this brief study was to identify an approach that would enable Christians and Muslims to deepen the conversation on matters pertaining to their faith. The conversation and mutual appraisal, we argued, are extremely important because of the changing realities of our time and the religiously plural context in which we now live. Gone are the days of monolithic communities. Plurality is an irretrievable fact of our modern life. Therefore, finding ways to maintain the integrity of our faith amidst the plurality is a major task. However, Christians cannot afford the luxury of thinking that the other religious communities will eventually go out of existence. These other religions, like Christianity, have been sustaining the spiritual life of millions for centuries. In fact, we find that there is growth and vitality in some of these other religious communities at rates that outpace Christianity, especially in western countries. The era of Christendom has ended and the pre-eminence of the Christian faith is no longer an unchallenged assumption.

The demise of Christian pre-eminence has given denominations and other communal expressions of the Christian faith an opportunity to search themselves to discover whether they have the resources to cope with life in a plural context. As the examination of the Moravian Communion has demonstrated, when a Christian community sets itself to engage the plural context, it can unearth aspects of its history that provide helpful resources for the task. The reflection on Islam from the point of view of the Moravian Church illustrates that finding ways to engage the plural context is a mandatory task for each self-conscious community. The examination has also shown that resources available to the Christian community are located in a multiplicity of communions and that there has to be a willingness to share these resources.

A pleasant finding of the study is that the Bohemian formula, which has traditionally been used in inter-church conversation, has some applicability in an interfaith context. Using the formula, we were able to explore those things that Christians and Muslims consider essential to their faith. We have seen that even with the differences within Islam, there seems to be the general affirmation that the oneness of God, the apostolic role of the Prophet Muhammad and the Qur'an are central to the faith and can be affirmed across the whole spectrum of Islamic piety. Among the things that Christians consider central to what it means to be a Christian, three affirmations stand out: the authority of the Bible, as the deposit of the saving message of salvation, the affirmation of Jesus, as Saviour and Lord and the necessity of Christian service (*diakonia*) in the world.

With the application of the Bohemian Formula, *in essentials unity, in non-essentials liberty, in all things charity*, in the context of their different affirmations, Christians and Muslims are faced with three challenges. The first is to consider whether there is any basis in their different affirmations for the confession of unity between the two religious traditions. Despite the protestation of Christian and Muslim scholars alike, our study has suggested that Christians and Muslims can say that they are at one in their ignorance of God, even with the revelations to which they can point. On the one hand, while the revelation of Jesus has revealed all that is needed for our salvation, Christians cannot thereby claim that they know God in God's absolute fullness. The writer of 1 Corinthians for example, alludes to the fact that there is still more that we will know. He writes, "for we see through a glass darkly." [1 Cor 13: . . .] On the other hand, Muslims do not claim that the Qur'an has revealed who God is in God's absolute fullness, though they do affirm that the Qur'an delineates the way we ought to live. Muslims will therefore readily admit that they are still ignorant of God because the human mind cannot fully comprehend God. It brings no shame then for Christians and Muslims to say that when it comes to knowledge of God we do not know everything. Muslims and Christians are at one in ignorance of the fullness of the divine life: in other words: in ignorance—unity! This willingness to admit ignorance we call the theology of modesty but it can also be seen as essential for growth in both the Christian and the Islamic faith.

If Christians and Muslims in modesty admit ignorance in their knowledge of God, despite revelations available to them, what can they say of each other? This is the second challenge arising from the application of the Bohemian formula. It is clear that there are differences, some of which run very deep, between the two faith communities. However, our study has shown that there is some overlap in the use of the traditions and stories and that Islam would have received these from Christian sources. For example, the account of Jesus in the Qur'an show some reliance on Christian sources, even though a different account of the fate of Jesus is given in the Bible. The Qur'an also makes extensive references to Mary, for which, again, the Biblican narrative and the Christian tradition would have been the primary sources. Islam also shares with Christianity and Judaism a fair amount of material that we find in the Hebrew Bible (or Old Testament), especially in relation to Abraham, Moses and some of the prophets. So, even if we cannot claim similarities between the Christian and Muslim traditions, we can certainly claim proximity. Although the Qur'an does not proclaim the death of Jesus, the fact that Muslims, like Christians, expect that Jesus will return means that Christians and Muslims can say that their respective faith traditions are near to each other. In other words: in faith–proximity!

The third challenge that the Bohemian Formula puts to Christians and Muslims is to be bold in stating their non-negotiable affirmations, while maintaining their mutual love. Muslims will not negotiate the role of the Qur'an in their piety, in the same way that Christians will not negotiate on the centrality of Jesus, their Saviour and Lord. Had the Qur'an related an account of Jesus that was closer to the Biblical account, Christian perception of Islam would be less antagonistic. The christological claims of Christians, especially as it relates to the doctrine of the Trinity, is also something that Muslims see as threatening the affirmation of the oneness in Allah. The most theologically contradictory claims between the two communities, then, relate to the person of Jesus. The differences will not be overcome through debate because the perceptions go to the very root of the way in which the believers understand themselves. So, on one hand, Christians cannot deny that the Qur'an speaks with much respect and favour about Jesus but from the point of view of the longest and most respected Christian tradition they must differ from the qur'anic presentation of Jesus. On the other hand, if Muslims were to accept all Christians claim about Jesus, they would become Christians and thereby surrender the pre-eminence they ascribe to the Qur'an. Reconciliation of these differences about the person of Jesus should not be expected. Christians and Muslims have to affirm that when it comes to Jesus there are major differences. In other words, in christology—difference!

With the claim of unity in ignorance, proximity in faith and difference in christology that they can make together, Christians and Muslims have not thereby solved all the problems of the relationship between them. Nevertheless, we have been able to show that Christians can give an account of Islam in terms of the fundamentals of their own faith, with the help of the formula, "in essentials, unity; in non-essentials, liberty; in all things charity." This way of accounting, the Muslim-Christian Research Group has argued, is necessary for relationship between the two faith traditions. Furthermore, we have shown that the posture of modesty provides a better atmosphere for conversation between the two communities. An attitude of modesty does not result in collision and stalemate in theological discourse.

The theological and methodological resources for interfaith dialogue the Moravian tradition offers the Christian tradition can provide the basis for a new development in theology, a theology of modesty.

Select Bibliography

Ariarajah, S. Wesley. *Not Without My Neighbour: Issues in Interfaith Relations* (Geneva: WCC Publications, 1999).

Avis, Paul, Ed. *Divine Revelation* (London: Darton, Longman, Todd, 1987).

Blanford, J. H. "In Essentials, Unity; in non-Essentials, Liberty; in All Things, Charity," *The Moravian Messenger*, Vol. XL No II (November 1930): 125–126.

Brown, Stuart, Ed. *Meeting in Faith: Twenty Years of Christian-Muslim Conversation Sponsored by the WCC* (Geneva: WCC Publications, 1989).

——. *The Nearest in Affection: Towards a Christian Understanding of Islam*. (Geneva: WCC Publications, 1994).

Cracknell, Kenneth. *Justice Courtesy & Love: Theologians and Missionaries Encountering World Religions* (London: Epworth Press, 1965).

Cragg, Kenneth. *The Event of the Qur'an: Islam in Scripture* (London: George Allen and Unwin Ltd., 1971).

——. *The Call of the Minaret* (London: Collins, 1986).

Crews, C. Daniel. *Confessing Our Unity in Christ: Historical and Theological Background to "The Ground of Unity"* (Winston Salem, NC: Moravian Archives, 1994).

Daniel, Norman. *Islam and the West: The Making of an Image* (Oxford: One World, 1993).

D'Costa, Gavin. *Theology and Religious Pluralism: The Challenge of Other Religions* (Oxford and New York: Basil Blackwell Inc., 1986).

——. *The Meeting of Religions and the Trinity* (Edinburgh: T & T Clarke, 2000).

Dupuis, Jacques, S. J. *Toward a Christian Theology of Religious Pluralism* (Maryknoll, NY: Orbis Books, 1997).

Eaton, Charles, le Gai. *Islam and the Destiny of Man* (London: George Allen and Unwin, 1985).

Esack, Farid. *Qur'an Liberation & Pluralism: An Islamic Perspective of the Interreligious Solidarity Against Oppression* (Oxford: Oneworld, 1997).

——. "Muslims Engaging the Other and the Humanum," Witte, John, and Martin, Richard, C., Eds. , *Sharing the Book: Religious Perspective on the Rights and Wrongs of Proselytism* (Maryknoll, NY: Orbis Books, 1999), 118–141.

Flesseman-van Leer, Ellen, Ed. *The Bible and Its Authority and Interpretation in the Ecumenical Movement* (Geneva: WCC, 1980).

Forell, George, Ed. *Nicholas Ludwig Count von Zinzendorf Bishop of the Moravian Brethren: Nine Public Lectures on Important Subjects in Religion: Preached in Fetter Lane Chapel London in the Year 1746* (Iowa City: University of Iowa Press, 1973).

Goddard, Hugh. *Christians & Muslims: From Double Standard to Mutual Understanding* (Richmond, Great Britain: Curzon Press, 1995).

Guillaume, Alfred. *Islam* (London: Penguin Books, 1956).

Haight, Roger. *Jesus Symbol of God* (Maryknoll, NY: Orbis Books, 1999).

Hamilton, J. Taylor. *A History of the Church Known as the Moravian Church of Unitas Fratrum or Unity of the Brethren: during the Eighteenth and Nineteenth Centuries* (Bethlehem, PA: Times Publishing Company, 1900).

Hasse, E. R. "Consider the Days of Old," *Moravian Messenger* Vol. XVIII (1908): 74–77.

Heim, S. Mark. *Salvations: Truth and Difference in Religion* (Maryknoll, NY: Orbis Books, 1995).

——, Ed. *Grounds for Understanding: Ecumenical Resources for Responses to Religious Pluralism* (Grand Rapids, Michigan: Wm B. Eerdmans, 1998).

Heymann, Frederick, G. *John Zizka and the Hussite Revolution* (Princeton, NJ: Princeton University Press, 1955).

Hick, John. *The Rainbow of Faiths* (London: SCM, 1995).

Hick, John and Brian Hebblewaithe, Eds. *Christianity and the Other Religions* (Glasgow: Collins, 1980).

Hick, John & Paul Knitter, Eds. *The Myth of Christian Uniqueness: Toward a Pluralistic Theology of Religions* (Maryknoll, NY: Orbis Books, 1997).

Kimball, Charles. *Striving Together: A Way Forward in Christian-Muslim Relations* (Maryknoll, NY: Orbis Books, 1991).

Kinnamon, Michael, & Brian Cope, Eds. *The Ecumenical Movement: An Anthology of Key Texts and Voices* (Geneva: WCC Publications, 1997).

Knitter, Paul. *No Other Name?: A Critical Survey of Christian Attitudes Towards the World Religions* (London: SCM, 1995).

Kung, Hans. *Christianity and the World Religions: Paths of Dialogue with Islam, Hinduism and Buddhism* (London: Collins, 1987).

Lewis, Bernard. *The Muslim Discovery of Europe* (New York and London: W. W. Norton & Co., 1982).

Lindbeck, George, A. *The Nature of Doctrine: Religion and Theology in a Post-Liberal Age* (London: SPCK, 1984).

Lossky, Nicholas, et al, Eds. *Dictionary of the Ecumenical Movement* (Geneva: WCC, 1991).

Mahmud, Abdel, H. *The Creed of Islam* (London: World of Islam Festival Trust, 1978).

May, John, D. "Essence—Identity—Liberation: Three Ways of Looking at Christianity," *Religious Tradition* # 6 (1984): 30–41.

Maynard, G. Oliver. *The Moravian Church Among the Churches: Pioneer in the Oe-cumenical Task* (Barbados: Cedar Press, 1982).

Mohammed, Ovey, N., S. J. *Muslim-Christian Relations: Past, Present, Future* (Mary-knoll, NY: Orbis Books, 1999).

Muslim-Christian Research Group, Translated by S. E. Brown. *The Challenge of Scrip-ture: the Bile and the Qur'an* (Maryknoll, NY: Orbis Books, 1989).

Nazir-Ali, Michael. *Islam: A Christian Perspective* (Exeter, UK: Paternoster House, 1983).

Nasr, Sayyed, H. "Islamic Christian Dialogue: Problems and Obstacles to be Pondered and Overcome," *Islam and Christian-Muslim Relations* Vol. 11 (2000): 214–227.

Nelson, Vernon. "The Slogan 'in essentials unity, in non-essentials liberty, in all things charity'." An unpublished paper in the Archives at Bethlehem Pennsylvania.

——. "A Translation of John Amos Comenius' *Unum Necessarium*," unpublished thesis presented to Moravian College Bethlehem, Pennsylvania, 1958.

Parrinder, Geoffrey. *Jesus in the Qur'an* (Oxford: Oneworld Publications, 1995).

Pulcini, Theodore. *Exegesis as Polemic Discourse: Ibn Hazim on Jewish and Christ-ian Scriptures* (Atlanta, Georgia: Scholars Press, 1998).

Rahner, Karl. *The Trinity* (Kent: Burns & Coats, 1970).

Rican, Rudolf. *The History of the Unity of the Brethren: A Protestant Hussite Church in Bohemia and Moravia*, trans. by D. Crews (Bethlehem, PA: Moravian Church in America, 1992).

Rippin, Andrew, & Jan Knappert, Eds. *Islam* (Chicago: Chicago University Press, 1986).

——. *Muslims: Their Religious Beliefs and Practices, Vol. 1: The Formative Period* (London, New York: Routledge, 1990).

Robinson, Francis. *Cambridge Illustrated History of the Islamic World* (Cambridge: Cambridge University Press, 1996).

Robinson, N. *Christ in Islam and Christianity: The Representation of Jesus in the Qur'an and the Classical Muslim Commentaries* (London: Macmillan Press, 1991).

Rouse, Ruth, et al, Eds. *A History of the Ecumenical Movement 1517–1968* (Geneva: WCC Publication, 1993).

Schimmel, Ann-Marie. *Deciphering the Signs of God: A Phenomenological Approach to Islam* (New York: New York State University Press, 1994).

Stanton, H. U. W. *The Teaching of the Qur'an* (London: Darf Publishers, 1987).

Stubenrauch, Bertram. "Controversy About the Incarnation: What is Specific to Christianity," *Irish Theological Quarterly* Vol. 64/4 (1999): 349–360.

Swartz, Merlin, L., Ed. *Studies in Islam* (New, Oxford: Oxford University Press, 1981).

Sykes, Stephen. *The Identity of Christianity: Theologians and the Essence of Chris-tianity from Schleiermacher to Barth* (London: SPCK, 1984).

Watt, W. Montgomery. *Islam Philosophy and Theology: An extended Survey* (Edin-burgh: Edinburgh University Press, 1985).

——. *Muslim-Christian Relations: Perceptions and Misperceptions* (London, New York: Routledge, 1991).

——. *Islamic Creeds: A Selection* (Edinburgh: Edinburgh University Press, 1994).

Whaling, Frank. "Scripture and Its Meanings: A Comparative Perspective Scriptures as Texts—Or More," *Studies in World Christianity* Vol. 6.1 (2000): 78–90.

Index

Abdullah, Yasuf Ali, 61, 80n23
absolute truth, 5, 71, 72, 78
accidentals, xiii, 20
adham, 27, 28
Africa, 50, 74, 75
Allah, 27, 29, 31, 37, 71, 85; attributes
    of, 27; daughters of, 137
Apology, The Moravian, 10, 55, 56
Arabian: inscription, 37n17; Prophet,
    49n4
Arabic, 13, 26, 27, 29, 34, 35
Augsburg Confession, 4, 8n10, 16, 17,
    52, 73
Augustine, 11, 12, 22n13, 23, 80n18
auxiliary, 2, 3, 10, 11, 12, 15, 20

Barth, Karl, 2, 54, 56, 80n18
Bohemian: Brethren, 4, 20, 62n3;
    confession, 4
bombing, 41, 42
Book of Order, 18, 52, 59
Brethren Unity, 17–18, 19
Buddhism, 75, 37n18
Byzantine Empire, 38n26, 41

Catholic (Roman), 16, 20, 26, 33, 47,
    53, 78; Catholicism, xii, 43, 53, 77
Christian: communions, xi, xii, 7, 31,
    52, 53; community, 5, 7, 16, 25, 43,

52; self-understanding, 7, 47, 48, 53,
    61, 62
christocentric, 16, 58, 63n31
christocentrism, 56, 57
christology: Moravian, 59, 79; Qur'anic,
    32, 78, 79 82n66
Church Order, 4, 7, 9, 53, 54, 69
Comenius, John Amos, 14–15, 32–35,
    36n34, 76
confessions, 4, 15, 25
creeds: Apostles', 26; Islamic, 38n23,
    40; Nicene, 25, 26, 45, 47, 62n3

denominations, xi, 51, 83;
    Denominationalism, 81
dialogue: ecumenical, 20; interfaith, xiii,
    1, 5, 21, 65, 68
diversity, 14, 17, 18
divine mystery, 17, 19, 31, 52, 56, 71
doctrinal system, 7, 13, 31, 39, 53

ecclesiology, xii, xiii, 3, 17, 19, 77
ecumenical movement, 19, 54, 66
Enlightenment, xiii, 5, 35, 54, 56, 81
evangelism, 74, 75, 81n48
exclusivenss, 26, 47; exclusivism, 1, 48

feminist christology, 78
Five Pillars (of Islam), 27

91

formulations (Doctrinal), 25, 65, 68, 78
Four Califs, 41

Gabriel (Angel), 42
gnosticism, 68
Godhead, 57, 58, 64n43, 80n19
God the Father, 3, 18, 31, 56, 57, 64
Ground of Unity (Moravian), 18, 19, 52

hadith, 48
Hanbalites, 34
harmony, xivn1, 6, 66, 76
hermeneutics, 4, 44, 54, 69, 80
Holy Spirit, xiii, 8n10, 18, 45, 56, 64, 70
humanist, 14, 15
Hus, John, 1, 12, 22n10, 53, 54; Hussite Movement, 53, 62n5

incarnation, 6, 31, 47, 56, 64n44, 69, 77
inculturated christology, 78
infallibility, 55, 63n21
interfaith theology, 7
iqra, 34

John of Damascus, 32
Joint Working Group (Roman Catholic and the World Council of Churches), 20
Judaism, 27, 30, 41, 47, 75, 85
justice, 21, 61, 66

kalima (word), 78
Knitter, Paul, 1, 25, 64n50, 77, 78
Kung, Hans, 32, 43, 46

liberation, 25, 46, 78
Longer Catechism, 25
Lukas of Prague, 13
Lutheran Reformation, xii, 3, 10, 13, 53

Mecca, 29, 30, 37n17, 40
Medina, 30, 40

monotheism, xiv, 13, 29, 30, 37n16, 43
Moravian: theology, 9, 11, 14, 17, 18, 58; Unity, 16, 17
Muslim self-understanding, 5, 22, 27, 48, 61, 79
Mu'tazilites, 34
mutual understanding, xi, 37n19

non-negotiable (doctrines), 26, 27, 43, 85

oneness (unicity) of God, 27, 30, 32, 48, 61, 84
orthodox, xii, 30, 31, 32, 43, 78; orthodoxy, 25, 26, 81n44
Ottoman Empire, xiii

pietism, 16, 56
pillars of belief, 27
pluralism, 1, 7, 33, 42, 69
polytheism, 27, 29, 30, 43
praxis, 25, 26, 39
prophethood, 42, 43, 71, 72

recite (Qur'an), 34, 36, 72
religions of the Book, 41, 55

sacraments, xiii, 3, 11, 12, 13, 14
salvation, xiii, 11, 14, 40, 55, 68, 84
Saviour, 6, 57, 58, 73, 85
scholasticism, 12
September 11, ix
seventeenth century, xii, 2, 15, 56, 76
Shahadah, 21, 27, 30, 39, 40
Sha'ri, 27, 48
Shiite, 66
Sufis, 40
Sunna, 42
Sunni, 37n7, 40, 66

theology: of modesty, 67–68, 69, 72, 84, 86; of Zinzendorf, 68, 69, 81
Thirty-Nine Articles, 25, 62n3
trinitarian, 31, 32, 58

Trinity, 6, 30–33, 42, 57, 73, 85. *See also* Trinitarian
tropus, 17; tropuses, 3, 4

ummi (illiterate), 34, 38n42, 72
uncreated (Qur'an), 34
Unitas Fratrum (Moravian Church), 1, 9, 12, 18–19, 53, 60
Unitatis Redingratio, xvn2
unity, 4, 6, 13, 15, 20; of the Brethren, 2, 13; synod, 10
unum necessarium, 15, 23n41

Vatican Council, xii, 4, 11, 20, 47
vessel (or Allah), 34, 72

violence, 28, 4
The Virgin Ma

The West, ix, 3:
Word of God, x
World Council c 20
world religion, 3' 82n67
worship, x, 6, 21,

Zinzendorf, 4, 16-; 79–81
Zizka, John, 62n5
Zwingli, 13